Ajit Singh

∩ח⊐ROIⴷ

Application Development

{ With Java Support }

Android Application Development

Notice of Rights

Notice of Liability

Ajit Singh

PREFACE

Android Application Development { With Java Support } is a great resource for developers/students who want to understand Android app development but who have little or no experience with mobile software/Applications. This book is about using Android Studio to understanding and implementing navigation patterns. This is a good book for those who want to learn Android from scratch. For those who do not know what to expect or whether you want to learn Android or not, this book could be the starting point.

The book is detailed and covers all the important concepts for you to build android apps. Even if you do have some experience, you will learn a lot of new stuff from this book. The book covers all essential concepts of Android from activity, services, Intent, fragments, views and database Connectivity, etc. There are many code samples that help you understand the UI design easily, which is otherwise a difficult. New features are covered in depth, and the knowledge that the book is geared to cover everything from introduction of a concept to learning how to implement it into your app makes this a great choice for new developers who are ready to make the jump into Android development.

This book is well written and fulfills the requirements of developers, project managers, educators, and students in developing fully featured Android applications and recommended to anyone who wants to focus on developing apps through a step -by-step and easy-to-understand approach. This is the useful real-world guide to building robust, commercial-grade Android apps with the new Android SDK/API, Android Studio, and latest development best practices. Bigger, better, and more comprehensive than ever, this book covers everything you need to start developing apps for modern Android devices. If you are serious about Android development, this book will prepare you to build virtually any app you can imagine!

This book is featured with;

- Updated coverage of the latest Android APIs, tools, utilities, and best practices.
- New coverage of the Android permission model.
- Activity, Service, Intent, View/Layout.
- ContentProvider.
- Powerful techniques for integrating material design into your apps.
- An all-new CHAPTER on using styles and reusing common UI components.
- Extensive new coverage of app design.
- Architecture, and backward compatibility.
- Database Connectivity.

Are you keen to get started building Android apps, but don't know where to start? Android Application Development is a comprehensive book to Build Android Apps with Java that will help kick-start your Android development practice.

CONTENTS

CHAPTER 5: ANDROID PROJECT STRUCTURE AND BASICS

- Android Project Structure
- Android Project Files
- Android Application Modules
- Types of Modules
- Project Structure Settings
- Anatomy of an Android Application
- Important Android Terminology
- Basic Android API Packages
- Android Advanced API Package

CHAPTER 6: ANDROID MANIFEST FILE

- Components of Manifest File
- Package Name and Application ID
- App Components
- Permissions
- Device Compatibility
- File Conventions
- Manifest Elements Reference
- Example of Manifest File

CHAPTER 7: WORKING WITH ACTIVITIES

- What is Activity?
- Configuring the AndroidManifest.xml File
- Life Cycle of an Activity
- Understanding Life Cycle of an Activity
- Context
- Activity Transition

CHAPTER 8: WORKING WITH SERVICES

- Use of Services
- Creating a Service
- Start and Stop Service
- Service Life Cycle
- Creating your own Service

CHAPTER 9: WORKING WITH INTENT

- Intent Structure
- Other Operations on Intent
- Types of Intent
- Intent Resolution

- Example of Intent
- Explanation of Example
- Standard Activity Actions
- Standard Broadcast Actions

CHAPTER 10: PERMISSIONS IN ANDROID

- Permission Approval
- Request Prompts for Dangerous Permissions
- Permission for Optional Hardware Features
- Custom App Permission
- Permission Protection Level
- How to View App's Permission?

CHAPTER 11: APPLICATION RESOURCES

- What are Resources?
- Resource Directory Hierarchy
- Resource Value Types
- Storing Different Resource Value Types
- Accessing Resource Programmatically
- Referencing System Resources

CHAPTER 12: USER INTERFACE SCREEN ELEMENTS

- Introduction to Views, Controls
- TextView
- EditText
- AutoCompleteTextView
- Spinner
- Buttons
- Check Boxes
- Radio Groups
- Pickers
- ImageView
- Adapter
- Android Custom ListView with Image and Text
- Android GridView
- Styles & Themes
- Menu
- Playing Media
- Shared Preferences

CHAPTER - 1

The Android Platform

Android - one of the most widely used operating systems for smartphones and tablets. Did you ever imagine how easy it is to chat with your friends on WhatsApp? Or did you ever imagine how easily you can book your food through Zomatto? Now the question arises of how these applications are developing and why on Android?

"A large section of the total users in the world use android."

- It is an operating system for smart phones
- It has an integrated Java virtual Machine
- It is based on Linux kernel
- System Interfaces are exposed through Java libraries

Figure 1a: About Android

Android is an open-source operating system based on Linux with a Java programming interface for mobile devices such as Smartphone (Touch Screen Devices who supports Android OS) as well for Tablets too. Android system is also called as Android Open Source Project (AOSP), lead by Google. Google Android is a Mobile Operating System and Application Development Platform for smartphones and tablets devices.

7

Android was developed by the Open Handset Alliance (OHA), which is led by Google. The Open Handset Alliance (OHA) is a consortium of multiple companies like Samsung, Sony, Intel and many more to provide services and deploy handsets using the android platform.

Android is called as "the first complete, open, and free mobile platform":

- **Complete**: allows for rich application development opportunities.
- **Open**: It is provided through open source licensing.
- **Free**: Android applications are free to develop. Android applications can be distributed and commercialized in a variety of ways.

Google's Android operating system is a mobile-based open-source platform. Nowadays, most smartphones, tablets, televisions, and other devices like even your Fitbit run on android. Android is based on top of the Linux kernel (modified version). Android is a powerful operating system and it supports a large number of applications on Smartphones. These applications are more comfortable and advanced for users. The hardware that supports android software is based on the ARM architecture platform. The android is an open-source operating system that means that it's free and anyone can use it. Android has got millions of apps available that can help you manage your life one or another way and it is available at low cost in the market for that reason android is very popular. Since Android is open-source, anyone can download the source code, edit it according to his requirements, and launch his own custom ROM. As a result, Android is available for almost all devices, irrespective of the manufacturers.

It provides you with facilities like SDK (also known as the software development kit) to write your codes, debug them, and make awesome apps for every generation. Android itself being widely used across the world makes it essential for developers to choose android. There are other operating systems such as IOS, Tizen, etc. Most Apple smartphones use IOS as their mobile operating system. Most of the smartphones available in the market use Android as their operating system, making it available to more users. It is not just why android is so essential, but several Android features make android quite valuable for the current scenario.

The Android platform includes an operating system based upon the Linux kernel, a GUI, a web browser and end-user applications that can be downloaded. Although the initial demonstrations of Android featured a generic QWERTY smart phone and large VGA screen, the operating system was written to run on relatively inexpensive handsets with conventional numeric keypads.

What it is not?

Android is not:

A Java ME implementation: Android applications are written in the Java language, but they are not run within a Java ME virtual machine, and Java - compiled classes and executable will not run natively in Android.

Part of the Linux Phone Standards Forum or the Open Mobile Alliance: Android runs on an open-source Linux kernel, but, while their goals are similar, Android's complete software stack approach goes further than the focus of these standards, defining organizations.

Simply an application layer (like UIQ or S60): While Android does include an application layer, "Android" also describes the entire software stack encompassing the underlying operating system, the API libraries, and the applications themselves.

A mobile phone handset Android includes a reference design for mobile handset manufacturers, but there is no single "Android phone." Instead, Android has been designed to support many alternative hardware devices.

Google's answer to the iPhone: The iPhone is a fully proprietary hardware and software platform released by a single company (Apple), while Android is an open-source software.

Why Android?

There are so many reasons you should choose the Android platform for mobile application development.

- **Zero/negligible development cost**

  The development tools like Android SDK, JDK, and Eclipse IDE, etc. are free to download for the android mobile application development. Also, Google charges a small fee of $25, to distribute your mobile app on the Android Market.

- **Open Source**

  The Android OS is an open-source platform based on the Linux kernel and multiple open-source libraries. In this way, developers are free to contribute to or extend the platform as necessary for building mobile apps which run on Android devices.

- **Multi-Platform Support**

  In the market, there is a wide range of hardware devices powered by the Android OS, including many different phones and tablets. Even the development of android mobile apps can occur on Windows, Mac OS, or Linux.

- **Multi-Carrier Support**

  World wide a large number of telecom carriers like Airtel, Vodafone, Idea Cellular, AT&T Mobility, BSNL, etc. are supporting Android-powered phones.

- **Open Distribution Model**

  Android Market place (Google Play store) has very few restrictions on the content or functionality of an android app. So the developer can distribute their app through the Google Play store and as well other distribution channels like Amazon's app store.

History of Mobile Application Development

The Motorola DynaTAC 8000X was the first commercially available cell phone and it is of brick size. First-generation mobile were expensive, not particularly full featured and has Proprietary software. As mobile phone prices dropped, batteries improved, and reception areas grew, more and more people began carrying these handy devices. Customers began pushing for more features and more games. They needed some way to provide a portal for entertainment and information services without allowing direct access to the handset. Early phone have postage stamp-sized low-resolution screens and limited storage and processing power, these phones couldn't handle the data-intensive operations required by traditional web browsers. The bandwidth requirements for data transmission were also costly to the user.

Android has been with us for quite a while now. Here's a quick rundown of its history;

- Andy Rubin founded Android Inc in 2003. He's got Google backing at the time.
- In 2005, Google bought Android Inc.
- Android was officially given to Open source in 2007. Google turned it over to Open Handset Alliance.
- In 2008, Android 1.0 was released; we didn't get the dessert names yet.
- In 2009, the dessert names started with Cupcake (Android 1.1 – 1.5), followed by Donut (1.6), and then Eclair (2.0).
- From that point on, Android has seen a steady cadence of releases. The current version of Android, at the time of writing, is Android 12.

OPEN HANDSET ALLIANCE (OHA)

In their own words,the OHA represents the following: "A commitment to openness, a shared vision for the future, and concrete plans to make the vision a reality, to accelerate innovation in mobile and offer consumers a richer, less expensive, and better mobile experience". The OHA hopes to deliver a better mobile software experience for consumers by providing the platform needed for innovative mobile development at a faster rate and with higher quality than existing platforms, without licensing fees for either software developers or handset manufacturers.

Wireless Application Protocol

The Wireless Application Protocol (WAP) standard emerged to address above concerns. WAP was stripped-down version of HTTP. WAP browsers were designed to run within the memory and bandwidth constraints of the phone. Third-party WAP sites served up pages written in a mark-up language called Wireless Mark up Language (WML). The WAP solution was great for handset manufacturers and mobile operators. Phone users can access the news, stock market quotes, and sports scores on their phones. WAP fell short of commercial expectations due to following reasons and Critics began to call WAP "Wait and Pay."

- Handset screens were too small for surfing.

- WAP browsers, especially in the early days, were slow and frustrating.

- Reading a sentence fragment at a time, and then waiting seconds for the next segment to download, ruined the user experience, especially because every second of downloading was often charged to the user.

- Mobile operators who provided the WAP portal often restricted which WAP sites were accessible.

Proprietary Mobile Platforms

Writing robust applications with WAP, such as graphic-intensive video games, was nearly impossible.Memory was getting cheaper, batteries were getting better, and PDAs and other embedded devices were beginning to run compact versions of common operating systems such as Linux and Windows. A variety of different proprietary platforms emerged and developers are still actively creating applications for them. Some of the examples of proprietary mobile platform are:

- Palm OS (now Garnet OS).

- RIM BlackBerry OS.

- Java Micro Edition [Java ME].

- Binary Runtime Environment for Wireless (BREW).

- Symbian OS.

- OS X iPhone.

Each platform has benefits and drawbacks.

The Android Platform

Most Android platform development is completed by Rubin's team at Google, where he acts as VP of Engineering and manages the Android platform roadmap. Google hosts the Android open source project and provides online Android documentation, tools, forums, and the Software Development Kit (SDK) for developers. All major Android news originates at Google.

Frameworks for Android Development

There are many tools available for Android development. Some of the best Android development tools are listed below:

Figure-1b

1. Corona SDK

This tool helps us to build 2-D applications. Moreover, it uses the Lua language, which is simple than C/C++. Game developers mostly use this framework.

2. Android Studio

Android Studio is the official IDE for Android application development. Also, it helps to build high-quality applications. Android beginners are recommended this application.

3. Phone – Gap

Adobe and Apache sponsor this framework. Moreover, it allows the users to keep watch on changes made while working and running programs.

4. Geny – Motion

Geny Motion helps us to develop and test applications in a faster and safer environment and it uses OpenGL which helps applications to run efficiently.

5. App Builder

Using this framework, users with no coding skills can build applications and web apps and also, it uses a drag and drop interface to create applications.

Allowed Programming Languages

The vast majority of Android applications are written exclusively in Java. However, there are other options as well:

- You can write parts of the app in C/C++. It is usually done for performance gains or porting over existing application's code bases etc.
- You can write an entire applications in C/C++. It is mostly done for games using OpenGL for 3D animations.
- You can write part of an android app in HTML, CSS, and JavaScript as well. There are tools which will package them into an Android application.

But still the fact is that Java is most used and popular language to build android applications. If you want to deep dive into android app development, then there is no excuse for not learning java.

Types of Android Devices

Android devices come in all shapes, sizes, and colors. However, there are three dominant "form factors":

- **Phone**
- **Tablet**
- **Television**

However, it is important that you understand that android has no built-in concept of a device being a "phone" or a "tablet" or a "TV". Rather, android distinguishes devices based on capabilities and features. So, you will not see an isPhone() method anywhere, though you can ask android:

What is the screen size?

does the device have telephony capability? etc.

Similarly, as you build your applications, rather than thinking of those three form factors, focus on what capabilities and features you need. Not only will this help you line up better with how android wants you to build your apps, but it will make it easier for you to adapt to other form factors that will come about such as:

- watches and other types of wearable devices.
- airplane seat-back entertainment centers.
- in-car navigation and entertainment devices etc.

Features of Android

1. Voice-search

This feature lets the user search by recording the voice message instead of typing it. Example - If we want to call XYZ person, we just have to speak and the call will be directed to the XYZ person, performing multi-tasking. With this feature, we can watch a video and also play games simultaneously.

2. Screen-capture

We can capture the screen using this feature.

3. Multiple Language Support

English is the default language but now we can use any local language. Also, Android supports multiple languages.

4. Gestures

With the help of gestures, we can use the phone without even touching it.

5. Tethering

With this feature, we can share internet connections through the wired/wireless hotspot.

6. Media Support

Android supports the following media H.263, H.264, MPEG-4, AMR, AMR-WB, AAC, HE-AAC, MP3, JPG, PNG, etc.

7. Storage

SQLite is an open-source relational database that is inbuilt in Android.

8. Auto-correct

This feature suggests words and corrects grammatical mistakes.

9. Sensors

Almost, every mobile phone has inbuilt sensors that sense the motion of the phone. Some of the inbuilt sensors are an accelerometer, heart rate, magnetic field sensor, gyroscope.

There are many such features provided by Android and with updates, we get new features every year.

The Android Version

Android is the operating system for powering screens of all sizes. Android version is named after a dessert. The latest version of android is Android 13. Following table shows how the android platform evolves.

Version	Name	Specifications	Level
1.0	Alpha	Web browser, Camera, Synchronization of Gmail, Contact and Calendar, Google Maps, Google Search, Google Talk, Instant Messaging, Text Messaging and MMS, Media Player, Notification, Voice Dialer, YouTube Video Player Other applications include: Alarm Clock, Calculator, Dialer (Phone), Home screen (Launcher), Pictures (Gallery), and Settings.	1
1.1	Beta	The update resolved bugs, changed the Android API and added a number of features such as Details and reviews available when a user searches for businesses on Maps, Ability to show/hide dial pad and save attachments in messages.	2

1.5	Cupcake	Virtual keyboards with text prediction and user dictionary for custom words, widgets, video recording and playback, Bluetooth, Copy and Paste, animated screen transition, auto rotation, upload video on YouTube, upload photo to Picasa.	3
1.6	Donut	Voice and text entry search, Multi-lingual speech synthesis, updated technology support for CDMA/EVDO, 802.1x, VPNs, and a text-to-speech engine, WVGA screen resolutions, Expanded Gesture framework and new Gesture Builder development tool	4
2.0 2.0.1 2.1	Éclair	Customize your home screen just the way you want it. Arrange apps and widgets across multiple screens and in folders. Stunning live wallpapers respond to your touch.	5 6 7
2.2-2.2.3	Froyo	Voice Typing lets you input text, while Voice Actions allow you to control your phone, just by speaking.	8
2.3	Gingerbread	New sensors make Android great for gaming – so you can touch, tap, tilt and play away.	9-10
3.0	Honeycomb	Optimized for tablets.	11-13
4.0	Ice Cream Sandwich	A new, refined design. Simple, beautiful and beyond smart.	14-15
4.1-4.3	Jelly Bean	Fast and smooth with slick graphics. With Google Now, you get just the right information at the right time.	16-18
4.4	Kit Kat	A more polished design, improved performance and new features.	19-20
5.0	Lolipop	Get the smarts of Android on screens big and small with the right information at the right moment.	21-22
6.0	Marshmallow	New App Drawer, Doze mode, Native finger print support, Android pay, USB type-C and USB 3.1 support, Direct share.	23

7.0	Nougat	Revamped notification, Split-screen use, file based encryption, direct boot, data saver	**24-25**
8.0	Oreo	Picture in picture, Google play protect, emoji	**26-27**
9.0	Pie	Adaptive Battery, adaptive brightness, intuitive navigation, dashboard, App timers, Wind down and do not disturb, Digital wellbeing.	**28**
10	Android 10 Q	Released Sept. 3, 2019. Abandoned the Back button in favor of a swipe-based approach to navigation. Introduced a dark theme and Focus Mode, which enables users to limit distractions from certain apps.	**29**
11	Android 11 Red Velvet Cake	Added built-in screen recording. Created a single location to view and respond to conversations across multiple messaging apps. This version also updated the chat bubbles so users can pin conversations to the top of apps and screens.	**30**
12	Android 12 Snow Cone	Added customization options for the user interface. The conversation widget let users store preferred contacts on their home screens. Added more privacy options, including sharing when apps access information such as camera, photos or microphone.	**31**
13	Android 13 Tiramisu	Included more customizable options including color, theme, language and music. Security updates included control over information apps can access, notification permission required for all apps and clearing of personal information on clipboard. This update enables multitasking by sharing of messages, chats, links and photos across multiple Android devices – including phones, tablets and Chromebooks.	**32-33**

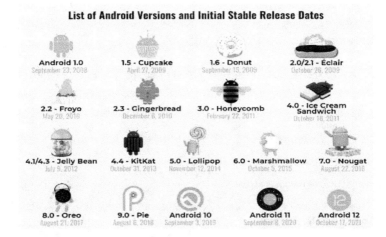

List of Android Versions and Initial Stable Release Dates

Android 1.0
September 23, 2008

1.5 - Cupcake
April 27, 2009

1.6 - Donut
September 15, 2009

2.0/2.1 - Éclair
October 26, 2009

2.2 - Froyo
May 20, 2010

2.3 - Gingerbread
December 6, 2010

3.0 - Honeycomb
February 22, 2011

4.0 - Ice Cream Sandwich
October 18, 2011

4.1/4.3 - Jelly Bean
July 9, 2012

4.4 - KitKat
October 31, 2013

5.0 - Lollipop
November 12, 2014

6.0 - Marshmallow
October 5, 2015

7.0 - Nougat
August 22, 2016

8.0 - Oreo
August 21, 2017

9.0 - Pie
August 6, 2018

Android 10
September 3, 2019

Android 11
September 8, 2020

Android 12
October 17, 2021

Figure 1c : Android Versions

Native Android Applications

Android phones will normally come with a suite of generic pre-installed applications that are part of the Android Open Source Project (AOSP), including, but not necessarily limited to:

- An e-mail client.
- An SMS management application.
- A full PIM (personal information management) suite including a calendar and contacts list.
- A WebKit-based web browser.
- A music player and picture gallery.
- A camera and video recording application.
- A calculator.
- The home screen.
- An alarm clock.

In many cases Android devices will also ship with the following proprietary Google mobile applications:

- The Android Market client for downloading third-party Android applications.
- A fully-featured mobile Google Maps application including Street View, driving directions and turn-by-turn navigation, satellite view, and traffic conditions.
- The Gmail mail client.
- The Google Talk instant-messaging client.
- The YouTube video player.

Android SDK Features

The true appeal of Android as a development environment lays in the APIs it provides. As an application-neutral platform, Android gives you the opportunities to create applications that areas much a part of the phone as anything provided out of the box. The following list highlights some of the most noteworthy Android features:

- No licensing, distribution, or development fees or release approval processes.
- Wi-Fi hardware access.
- GSM, EDGE, and 3G networks for telephony or data transfer, enabling you to make or receive calls or SMS messages, or to send and retrieve data across mobile networks.
- Comprehensive APIs for location-based services such as GPS.
- Full multimedia hardware control, including playback and recording with the camera and microphone.
- APIs for using sensor hardware, including accelerometers and the compass.
- Libraries for using Bluetooth for peer-to-peer data transfer.
- IPC message passing.
- Shared data stores.
- Background applications and processes.
- Home-screen Widgets, Live Folders, and Live Wallpaper.

- The ability to integrate application search results into the system search.

- An integrated open-source HTML5 WebKit-based browser.

- Full support for applications that integrate map controls as part of their user interface.

- Mobile-optimized hardware-accelerated graphics, including a path-based 2D graphics library and support for 3D graphics using OpenGL ES 2.0.

- Media libraries for playing and recording a variety of audio/video or still image formats.

- Localization through a dynamic resource framework.

- An application framework that encourages reuse of application components and the replacement of native applications.

Android Architecture

Android is an open source, Linux-based software stack created for a wide array of devices and form factors. The following diagram shows the major components of the Android platform.

The Linux Kernel

The foundation of the Android platform is the Linux kernel. For example, the Android Runtime (ART) relies on the Linux kernel for underlying functionalities such as threading and low-level memory management.Using a Linux kernel allows Android to take advantage of key security features and allows device manufacturers to develop hardware drivers for a well-known kernel.

The primary reason behind opting for the Linux kernel as the heart of the OS was that it provided certain core features:

1. Security: The kernel controls the security between the application and the system.

2. Memory: Manages memory with a high level of efficiency, thus providing the freedom to develop great apps.

3. Process Management: Appropriately delegates resources to processes whenever required.

4. Network Stack: Handles all the network communication.

5. Driver Model: Makes sure that the application works. Hardware manufacturers can build drivers into the Linux build.

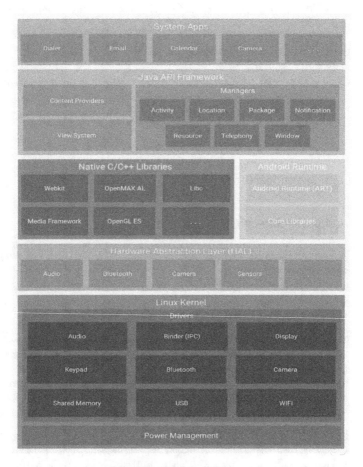

Figure-1d: Android Software Stack

Hardware Abstraction Layer (HAL)

The hardware abstraction layer (HAL) provides standard interfaces that expose device hardware capabilities to the higher-level Java API framework. The HAL consists of multiple library modules, each of which implements an interface for a specific type of hardware component, such as the camera or Bluetooth module.

When a framework API makes a call to access device hardware, the Android system loads the library module for that hardware component.

Android Runtime

For devices running Android version 5.0 (API level 21) or higher, each app runs in its own process and with its own instance of the Android Runtime (ART). ART is written to run multiple virtual machines on low-memory devices by executing DEX files, a byte code format designed especially for Android that's optimized for minimal memory footprint. Build tool chains, such as Jack, compile Java sources into DEX byte code, which can run on the Android platform.

Some of the major features of ART include the following:
- Ahead-of-time (AOT) and just-in-time (JIT) compilation.
- Optimized garbage collection (GC).
- On Android 9 (API level 28) and higher, conversion of an app package's format (DEX) files to more compact machine code.
- Better debugging support, including a dedicated sampling profiler, detailed diagnostic exceptions and crash reporting, and the ability to set watch points to monitor specific fields.

Prior to Android version 5.0 (API level 21), Dalvik was the Android runtime. If your app runs well on ART, then it should work on Dalvik as well, but the reverse may not be true. Android also includes a set of core runtime libraries that provide most of the functionality of the Java programming language, including some Java 8 language features that the Java API framework uses.

Native C/C++ Libraries

Many core Android system components and services, such as ART and HAL, are built from native code that requires native libraries written in C and C++. The Android platform provides Java framework APIs to expose the functionality of some of these native libraries to apps. For example, you can access OpenGL ES through the Android framework's Java OpenGL API to add support for drawing and manipulating 2D and 3D graphics in your app. If you are developing an app that requires C or C++ code, you can use the Android NDK to access some of these native platform libraries directly from your native code.

Android Libraries

Android libraries are Java-based libraries which are specific to Android development. Examples include the application framework libraries as well as those that facilitate user interface building and graphics drawing. Some of the key Android libraries available to the Android developer are:

1. android.app – Provides access to the application model and is the cornerstone of all Android applications.

2. android.content – Facilitates content access, publishing, and messaging between applications and application components.

3. android.database – Used to access data published by content providers and includes SQLite database management classes.

4. android.opengl – A Java interface to the OpenGL ES 3D graphics rendering API.

5. android.os – Provides applications with access to standard operating system services including messages, system services and inter-process communication.

6. android.text – Used to render and manipulate text on a device display.

7. android.view – The fundamental building blocks of application user interfaces.

8. android.widget – A rich collection of pre-built user interface components such as buttons, labels, list views, layout managers, radio buttons etc.

9. android.webkit – A set of classes intended to allow web-browsing capabilities to be built into applications.

Java API Framework

The entire feature-set of the Android OS is available to you through APIs written in the Java language. These APIs form the building blocks you need to create Android apps by simplifying the reuse of core, modular system components and services, which include the following:

- A rich and extensible View System you can use to build an app's UI, including lists, grids, text boxes, buttons, and even an embeddable web browser.
- A Resource Manager, providing access to non-code resources such as localized strings, graphics, and layout files.

- A Notification Manager that enables all apps to display custom alerts in the status bar.
- An Activity Manager that manages the lifecycle of apps and provides a common navigation back stack.
- Content Providers that enable apps to access data from other apps, such as the Contacts app, or to share their own data.

Developers have full access to the same framework APIs that Android system apps use.

System Apps

Android comes with a set of core apps for email, SMS messaging, calendars, internet browsing, contacts, and more. Apps included with the platform have no special status among the apps the user chooses to install. So a third-party app can become the user's default web browser, SMS messenger, or even the default keyboard (some exceptions apply, such as the system's Settings app). Android boasts a crazy amount of great features. Here are a few of them:

1. Android is open-source and developers can customize the OS based on requirements.

2. Supports connectivity for GSM, CDMA, WIFI, NFC, Bluetooth, etc. for telephony or data transfer. It will allow us to make or receive calls / SMS messages and we can send or retrieve data across mobile networks.

3. Pair with other devices through WiFi.

4. Android has multiple APIs to support location-based services such as GPS.

5. We can perform all data storage related activities by using lightweight database SQLite.

6. It has a wide range of media supports like AVI, MKV, FLV, MPEG4, etc. to play or record a variety of audio/video and various image formats like JPEG, PNG, GIF, BMP, MP3, etc.

7. It has extensive support for multimedia hardware control to perform playback or recording using camera and microphone.

8. It has an integrated open-source WebKit layout based web browser to support HTML5, CSS3.

9. Supports multitasking, we can move from one task window to another, and multiple applications can run simultaneously.

10. It allows you to reuse the application components and the replacement of native applications.

11. We can access the hardware components like camera, GPS, and accelerometer.

12. It has support for 2D/3D Graphics.

The system apps function both as apps for users and to provide key capabilities that developers can access from their own app. For example, if your app would like to deliver an SMS message, you don't need to build that functionality - you can instead invoke whichever SMS app is already installed to deliver a message to the recipient you specify.

Application Framework

The Android OS exposes the underlying libraries and features of the Android device that are using a Java API. This is what is known as the Android framework. The framework exposes a safe and uniform means to utilize Android device resources.

Figure-1e

1) Activity Manager

Applications use the Android activity component for presenting an entry point to the app. Android Activities are the components that house the user interface that app users interact with. As end-users interact with the Android device, they start, stop, and jump back and forth across many applications. Each navigation event triggers activation and deactivation of many activities in respective applications.

The Android ActivityManager is responsible for predictable and consistent behavior during application transitions. The ActivityManager provides a slot for app creators to have their apps react when the Android OS performs global actions. Applications can listen to events such as device rotation, app destruction due to memory shortage, an app being shifted out of focus, and so on.

Some examples of the way applications can react to these transitions include pausing activity in a game, stopping music playing during a phone call.

2) Window Manager

Android can determine screen information to determine the requirements needed to create windows for applications. Windows are the slots where we can view our app user interface. Android uses the Window manager to provide this information to the apps and the system as they run so that they can adapt to the mode the device is running on.

The Window Manager helps in delivering a customized app experience. Apps can fill the complete screen for an immersive experience or share the screen with other apps. Android enables this by allowing multi-windows for each app.

3) Location Manager

Most Android devices are equipped with GPS devices that can get user location using satellite information to which can go all the way to meters precision. Programmers can prompt for location permission from the users, deliver location, and aware experiences. Android is also able to utilize wireless technologies to further enrich location details and increase coverage when devices are enclosed spaces. Android provides these features under the umbrella of the Location-Manager.

4) Telephony Manager

Most Android devices serve a primary role in telephony. Android uses TelephoneManager to combine hardware and software components to deliver telephony features. The hardware components include external parts such as the sim card, and device parts such as the microphone, camera, and speakers. The software components include native components such as dial pad, phone book, ringtone profiles. Using the TelephoneManager, a developer can extend or fine-tune the default calling functionality.

5) Resource Manager

Android app usually come with more than just code. They also have other resources such as icons, audio and video files, animations, text files, and the like. Android helps in making sure that there is efficient, responsive access to these resources. It also ensures that the right resources are delivered to the end-users. For example, the proper language text files are used when populating fields in the apps.

6) View System

Android also provides a means to easily create common visual components needed for app interaction. These components include widgets like buttons, image holders such as ImageView, components to display a list of items such as ListView, and many more. The components are premade but are also customizable to fit app developer needs and branding.

7) Notification Manager

The Notification Manager is responsible for informing Android users of application events. It does this by giving users visual, audio or vibration signals or a combination of them when an event occurs. These events have external and internal triggers. Some examples of internal triggers are low-battery status events that trigger a notification to show low battery. Another example is user-specified events like an alarm. Some examples of external triggers include new messages or new wifi networks detected. Android provides a means for programmers and end-users to fine-tune the notifications system. This can help to guarantee they can send and receive notification events in a means that best suits them and their current environments.

8) Package Manager

Android also provides access to information about installed applications. Android keeps track of application information such as installation and uninstallation events, permissions the app requests, and resource utilization such as memory consumption. This information can enable developers to make their applications to activate or deactivate functionality depending on new features presented by companion apps.

9) Content Provider

Android has a standardized way to share data between applications on the device using the content provider. Developers can use the content provider to expose data to other applications. For example, they can make the app data searchable from external search applications. Android itself exposes data such as calendar data, contact data, and the like using the same system.

Android Runtime and Core/Native Libraries

1) Android Runtime

Android currently uses Android Runtime (ART) to execute application code. ART is preceded by the Dalvik Runtime that compiled developer code to Dalvik Executable files (Dex files). These execution environments are optimized for the android platform taking into consideration the processor and memory constraints on mobile devices. The runtime translates code written by programmers into machine code that does computations and utilizes android framework components to deliver functionality. Android hosts multiple applications and system components that each run in their processes.

Core Libraries

In this segment, we will discuss some of the core libraries that are present in the Android operating system.

Figure-1f

2) MediaFramework

Android also natively supports popular media codecs, making it easy for apps created on the Android platform to use/play multimedia components out of the box.

3) SQLite

Android also has an SQLite database that enables applications to have very fast native database functionality without the need for third party libraries.

4) Freetype

Android comes with a preinstalled fast and flexible font engine. This makes it possible for application developers to style components of their application and deliver a rich experience that communicates the developer's intent.

5) OpenGL

Android also comes with the OpenGL graphics system. It's a C library that helps Android use hardware components in the real-time rendering of 2D and 3D graphics.

6) SSL

Android also comes with an inbuilt security layer to enable secure communication between applications on Android and other devices such as servers, other mobile devices, routers.

31

7) SGL

Android comes with a graphics library implemented in low-level code that efficiently renders graphics for the android platform. It works with the higher-level components of the Android framework Android graphics pipeline.

8) Libc

The core of Android contains libraries written in C and C++, which are low-level languages meant for embedded use that help in maximizing performance. Libc provides a means to expose low-level system functionalities such as Threads, Sockets, IO, and the like to these libraries.

9) Webkit

This is an open-source Browser engine used as a basis to build browsers. The default Android browser before version 4.4 KitKat uses it for rendering web pages. It enables application developers to render web components in the view-system by using WebView. This enables apps to integrate web components into their functionality.

10) Surface Manager

The surface manager is responsible for ensuring the smooth rendering of application screens. It does this by composing 2D and 3D graphics for rendering. It further enables this by doing off-screen buffering.

Dalvik Virtual Machine (DVM)

As we know the modern JVM is high performance and provides excellent memory management. But it needs to be optimized for low-powered handheld devices as well. The **Dalvik Virtual Machine (DVM)** is an android virtual machine optimized for mobile devices. It optimizes the virtual machine for *memory, battery life* and *performance.* Dalvik is a name of a town in Iceland. The Dalvik VM was written by Dan Bornstein. The Dex compiler converts the class files into the .dex file that run on the Dalvik VM. Multiple class files are converted into one dex file. Let's see the compiling and packaging process from the source file:

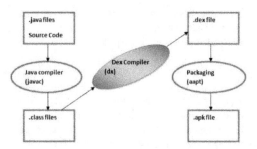

The javac tool compiles the java source file into the class file.

The **dx tool** takes all the class files of your application and generates a single .dex file. It is a platform-specific tool.

The **Android Assets Packaging Tool (aapt)** handles the packaging process.

Factors that affect Mobile Application development

You should keep in mind the following factors while developing mobile application:

- Low processing power.
- Limited RAM.
- Limited permanent storage capacity.
- Small screens with low resolution.
- High costs associated with data transfer.
- Slow data transfer rates with high latency.
- Unreliable data connections.
- Limited battery life.

Following are some of the factors that affect app development time:

- User Interface & User Experience.
- Custom application.
- Resource availability.
- App security and publishing the app.
- App designing.
- Number of screens / devices / platforms / operating systems.
- Third party integration.
- Features.
- Understanding the business logic.
- Complexity of the App.

Major Android Components

Remember when you started learning java, your first program was 'Hello World ' application. You wrote a main() method and some print statement; then some magic happened and output was written in console. Similarly, when you entered into web programming area, normally you will learn/write the http servlet first. You extend a class and write some code in it; and then something passes control to your servlet and it start executing.

Android takes the second approach i.e. you extend some specific classes and define your configuration in some XML file and you are good to start your first android app. The subclasses you create, by extending base classes supplied by Android, are called components. Below are major 4 components you should know before hand:

1) Activities

The major building block of the user interface is called activity. You can think of an activity as an user interface as you see in classic windows application. Just like in windows where an application takes most of screen apart from toolbar strip, activity also leave area on mobile device screen only for strip on top contain device clock, signal strength indicators etc. Remember this term, you will be using it in every step of your app development.

2) Services

Activities are short-lived and can be shut down at any time, such as when the user presses the BACK button or HOME button. Services, on the other hand, are designed to keep running, if needed, independent of any activity inside application, for a short period of time. You might use a service for checking for updates to an RSS feed, or to play back music even if the controlling activity (i.e. media player) is no longer operating on front screen.

3) Content Providers

Content providers provide a level of abstraction for any data stored on the device that is accessible by 'multiple' applications. The Android development model encourages you to make your own data available to other applications. Building a content provider lets you do that, while maintaining a degree of control over how your data gets accessed by other apps on same device.

4) Broadcast Receivers

The system, and/or other apps, will send out broadcasts/notifications from time to time for everything relevant e.g. for the battery is getting low, the screen turns off OR connectivity changes from WiFi to mobile data etc. A broadcast receiver in your application will be able to listen for these broadcasts/notifications and respond accordingly the way you want.

Key Terms Used in Android Development

a) Widgets

In Android terms, a widget is the "micro" unit of user interface. Fields, buttons, labels, lists, and so on are all widgets. Your activity's UI, therefore, is made up of one or more of these widgets. You can think of all text boxes, drop downs and other HTML UI elements in normal webpage. In Android, they are called widgets. Easy to remember.

b) Containers/ Layout Managers

If you have more than one widget — which is fairly typical — you will need to tell Android how those widgets are organized on the screen. To do this, you will use various container classes referred to as 'layout managers'. These will let you put things in rows, columns, or more complex arrangements as needed.

35

To describe how the containers and widgets are connected, you will typically create a layout resource file and put in project's resource folder from where android pick it up directly and render the whole UI for you automatically. In more familiar terms, they are equivalent to DIVs, SPANs or Table tags in HTML.

c) Resources

Resources in android refer to things like images, strings, and other similar things that your application uses on runtime. In android programming, you will be creating lot's of such resource files for providing data on runtime of application; more like properties files in normal java applications.

d) Fragments

Normally you will design your app in such a way that UI will work across all sorts of devices: phones, tablets, televisions, etc. For example, Gmail app on a tablet will show your list of labels, the list of conversations in a selected label, and the list of messages in a selected conversation, all in one activity (screen) in a tablet. However, same Gmail app on a phone cannot do that, as there is not enough screen space, so it shows each of those (labels, conversations, messages) in separate activities (screens). Android supplies a construct called the fragment to help make it easier for you to implement these sorts of effects. We will learn them in coming posts in detail.

e) Apps and Packages

Given a bucket of source code and a basket of resources, the Android build tools will give you an application as a result. The application comes in the form of an APK file. It is APK file that you will upload to the Play Store or distribute by other means.

Important thing to learn is that each android application has a unique package name and it must fulfill three requirements:

- It must be a valid java package name, as some java source code will be generated by the android build tools in this package.
- No two applications can exist on a device at the same time with the same package.
- No two applications can be uploaded to the Play Store having the same package.

So, you will pick a package name following the "reverse domain name" convention (e.g., in.ajitvoice.android.app). That way, the domain name system ensures that your package name prefix (in.ajitvoice) is unique, and it is up to you to ensure that the rest of the package name distinguishes one of your apps from any other.

Android Design Goals

The goals of the Android system are focused on the user experience in a mobile environment, using a touch screen and connecting to networks through either telephony (using 3G and 4G, as of this writing) or Wi-Fi.

We focused the design of Android around three overarching goals, which apply to our core apps as well as the system at large. As you design apps to work with Android, consider these goals:

- **Enchant Me**
- **Simplify My life.**
- **Make Me Amazing.**

Enchant Me: Android Apps are "Sleek & Aesthetically" pleasing on mobile levels. Transactions are "fast and clear". App icons are works of art in their own right. Your app's should be combine "beauty, simplicity" and purpose of creating a "Magical Experience".

Simplify My life: Android apps make life easier and are easy to understand. When people use your app's for the first time they should grasp the most important features people of all ages and cultures feel family in control.

Make Me Amazing: android apps empower people to try new things and to use app's in inventive new ways. Android lets people combine applications new work flows, multitasking notifications and share across app's. At the same time your app should feel personal, giving people access to superb technology with clarity and grace.

How Android works?

As I said Android uses Java for application development. So you can code your Android apps using Java API provided by Google, and it compiles them into class files. The similarity ends here, Android doesn't use Java Virtual machine (JVM) for executing class files, instead, it uses Dalvik virtual machine, which is not a true JVM and doesn't operate on Java bytecode. In order to run on Dalvik Virtual machines, class files are further compiled into Dalvik Executable or DEX format. After conversion to DEX format, class files along with other resources are bundled into Android Package (APK) for distribution and installation into various devices. The key thing to know is that Dalvik VM is based on a subset of the Apache Harmony Project for its core class library, which means it doesn't support all J2SE API. If you are using Eclipse IDE for coding Android Apps, then you don't need to worry much because it will help you with code completion.

Each Android App normally runs on its own virtual machine(VM). This implies that the app can run in isolation from other apps.

Android system applies the principle of least privilege. This means that each app will only have access to the components it requires to do its work, and no more.

However, there are ways for an app to share data with other apps, such as by sharing Linux user id between app, or apps can request permission to access device data like SD card, contacts etc.

Android 5.0 (Lollipop) and above have been using ART as the main runtime. ART was introduced experimentally in Android 4.4 KitKat. Before ART Runtime was DVM (Dalvik Runtime).

ART runtime utilizes AOT (Ahead Of Time) compilation. This compilation model involves optimizing application performance on startup and application execution. DVM utilizes JIT (Just In Time) compilation model. However, with AOT dex files are compiled during installation. This compilation is done using the dex2oat tool. Now let's see How Android Application runs on a device?

How Android apps run on Devices?

If you are familiar with Linux and the concept of process, then it's easy to understand how android applications run. By default, Each Android application is assigned a unique user id by the Android operating system. After starting an android application, they run in their own process, inside their own virtual machine.

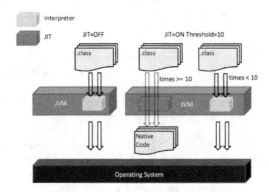

Figure 1h: Android Apps Running on Devices (Dalvik)

Android operating system manages the starting and shutting down the application process, whenever required. This means each android application runs in isolation with others, but they can certainly request access to hardware and other system resources.

If you are familiar with mobile application development, maybe in J2ME, then you may know about permissions. So when an android application is installed or started, it requests the necessary permission required to connect to the internet, phone book, and other system resources. The user explicitly provides grant these permissions, or it may deny. All these permissions are defined in the manifest file of the Android application. Unlike the Java Manifest file, the Android manifest is an XML file, which lists all the components of apps, and settings for those components.

Four major components of Android application development is Activities, Services, Content Providers, and Broadcast Receivers. Activity is most common of them, as it represents a single screen in Android Application. For example, in an Android Game, you can have multiple screens for login, high score, instructions, and game screen. Each of these screens represents different Activities inside your app.

Note: Dalvik is a discontinued process virtual machine (VM) in Android operating system that executes applications written for Android. (Dalvik bytecode format is still used as a distribution format, but no longer at runtime in newer Android versions.)

What makes up an Android App?

An Android app may, at first, seem like a desktop app, but it's not correct to think of them that way. Android apps are structurally different from desktop apps. A desktop app generally contains all the routines and subroutines it needs to run. It is self-contained. An Android app is quite different. It's made of loosely coupled components that are held together by a (uniquely Android) messaging system called Intents. The diagram below shows a logical representation of an Android app.

It's made up of components like Activities, Services, BroadcastReceivers, ContentProviders, and Intents.

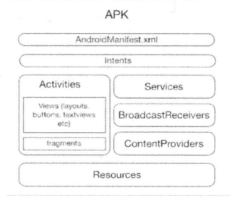

Figure 1i: representation-android-app

Activities

This component takes care of user interaction. It's where you put UI elements and where you capture user-generated events (e.g., click, long-clicks, swipes).

BroadcastReceivers

BroadcastReceivers are components that can listen for events (system or user-generated). If you want to perform a task in response to an event (e.g., Network went down, a phone call, somebody sending an SMS message, etc.), you can use BroadcastReceivers for that.

ContentProviders

ContentProviders lets you write apps that can share data with other apps. A good example of a ContentProvider is the "Contacts" app on Android. It can expose contact data to other apps without exposing the raw data store. It facilitates data sharing via API.

Services

If you need to run code in the background without freezing the user interface, you can use services. You can use these components to perform long-running tasks, e.g., downloading a large file, playing background music, etc.

Intents

Intents are used to activate components and to pass data from one component to another if you need to launch an Activity (a UI component) from another Activity (usually MainActivity) as a response to a user-event (like a button click, you will do that by creating an Intent object and launching it.

Manifest file

The Android Manifest is an XML file that describes the application, all its components, and restrictions (whether or not it can use the network/internet, use GPS, etc.). Don't worry if you're not too handy with XML files; this is usually generated when you create a new project. This file is also updated (automatically) as you add components to your project.

Why Java for Android application development?

If you want to get started with application development, Google provides a Java API to get started and compiles your files into classes. Why did Android prefer Java for its development platform? There are multiple reasons such as; Java is a commonly used language and many programmers know it, it can run on a virtual machine (VM) so no need to recompile for different phones, better security, many development tools available for Java, and Java is a known industry language with most phones compatible with it. Though Google provides the Java API, Android does not use JVM to execute class files. Rather, it uses Dalvik Virtual Machine (DVM). The class files are compiled into Dalvik Executable (DEX) format, and bundled as Android Package (APK) along with other resources.

XML & Java code

An XML file is used to build layouts in Android. Layouts are static pages(screens) that can be manipulated using java code (programmatically) Declaring Vis in XML enables us to better separate the presentation of our application from the code that controls its behavior.

CHAPTER - 2

Installing Android Studio

Android Studio is a popular IDE developed by JetBrains and Google, designed specifically for Android development. It's available for Windows, macOS, Linux, and Chrome OS. Android Studio is Google's officially supported IDE for developing Android apps. This IDE is based on IntelliJ IDEA, which offers a powerful code editor and developer tools. Android Studio includes the following features:

- A flexible Gradle-based build system.
- A fast and feature-rich emulator.
- A unified environment where you can develop for all Android devices.
- Instant Run to push changes to your running app without building a new APK.
- Code templates and GitHub integration to help you build common app features and import sample code.
- Extensive testing tools and frameworks.
- Lint tools to help you catch performance, usability, version compatibility, and other problems.
- C++ and NDK support.
- Built-in support for Google Cloud Platform, making it easy to integrate Google Cloud Messaging and Google App Engine.
- Plugin architecture for extending Android Studio via plugins.

Google provides Android Studio for the Windows, Mac OS X, and Linux platforms. You can download Android Studio from the Android Studio homepage, where you'll also find the traditional SDKs with Android Studio's command-line tools. Before downloading Android Studio, make sure your platform meets the following requirements.

System Requirements for Android Studio

- 64-bit Microsoft® Windows® 8/10/11.
- x86_64 CPU architecture; 2nd generation Intel Core or newer, or AMD CPU with support for a Windows Hypervisor.
- 8 GB RAM or more.
- 8 GB of available disk space minimum (IDE + Android SDK + Android Emulator).
- 1280 x 800 minimum screen resolution.

Downloading & Installing Android Studio

Download android studio from **http://developer.android.com/sdk/index.html.** It will open following web page. I launched android-studio-ide-181.5056338-windows.exe to start the installation process. The installer responded by presenting the Android Studio Setup dialog box shown in Figure 2b.

Figure-2a

Step 1
To download the Android Studio, visit the official Android Studio website in your web browser.

Step 2
Click on the "Download Android Studio" option.

Figure-2b

Step 3
Double click on the downloaded "Android Studio-ide.exe" file.

Figure-2c

Step 4
"Android Studio Setup" will appear on the screen and click "Next" to proceed.

Figure-2b

Step 5
Select the components that you want to install and click on the "Next" button.

Figure-2c

Step 6
Now, browse the location where you want to install the Android Studio and click "Next" to proceed.

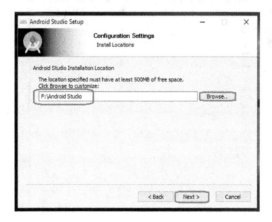

Figure-2d

Step 7
Choose a start menu folder for the "Android Studio" shortcut and click the "Install" button to proceed.

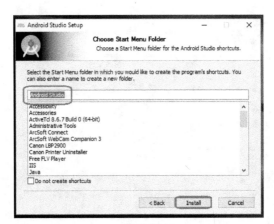

Figure-2e

Step 8
After the successful completion of the installation, click on the "Next" button.

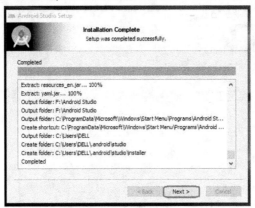

Figure-2f

47

Step 9

Click on the "Finish" button to proceed.

Figure-2g

Now, your Android studio welcome screen will appear on the screen.

Figure-2h

48

Android Studio Setup Configuration

Step 10
"Android Studio Setup Wizard" will appear on the screen with the welcome wizard. Click on the "Next" button.

Figure-2i

Step 11
Select (check) the "Standard" option if you are a beginner and do not have any idea about Android Studio. It will install the most common settings and options for you. Click "Next" to proceed.

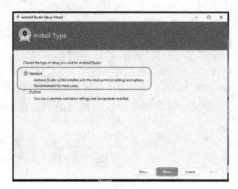

Figure-2j

Step 12

Now, select the user interface theme as you want. (I prefer Dark theme (Dracula) that is most liked by the coders). Then, click on the "Next" button.

Figure-2k

Step 13

Now, click on the "Finish" button to download all the SDK components.

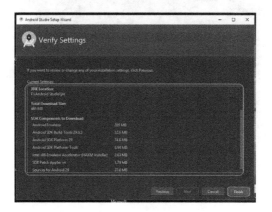

Figure-2l

And, the downloading and installation process of components gets started.

Figure-2m

Step 14
After downloading all the necessary components, click on the "Finish" button.

Figure-2n

Congrats, your Android Studio has been successfully installed in your system and you can start a new Android studio project.

Important Note: On some Windows systems, the launcher script does not find where Java is installed. If you encounter this problem, you need to set an environment variable indicating the correct location. Select Start menu > Computer > System Properties > Advanced System Properties. Then open Advanced tab > Environment Variables and add a new system variable JAVA_HOME that points to your JDK folder, for example C:\Program Files\Java\jdk1.7.0_XX.

Important Notes

- Android studio is a resource hungry program. You need to have patience while using it.

- Sometimes Android studio might download files from the internet, so keep your wifi Hotspot ready.

- In very rare cases, your firewall might block android studio.

- If your computer is slow, use USB debugging to use your phone as an AVD replacement.

- If you are using an old PC, make sure that the virtualization is turned on.

CHAPTER - 3
Android Studio

Android Studio is the official integrated development environment (IDE) for Android application development. It is based on the IntelliJ IDEA, a Java integrated development environment for software, and incorporates its code editing and developer tools.

To support application development within the Android operating system, Android Studio uses a Gradle-based build system, emulator, code templates, and Github integration. Every project in Android Studio has one or more modalities with source code and resource files. These modalities include Android app modules, Library modules, and Google App Engine modules. Android Studio uses an Instant Push feature to push code and resource changes to a running application. A code editor assists the developer with writing code and offering code completion, refraction, and analysis. Applications built in Android Studio are then compiled into the APK format for submission to the Google Play Store.

The software was first announced at Google I/O in May 2013, and the first stable build was released in December 2014. Android Studio is available for Mac, Windows, and Linux desktop platforms. It replaced Eclipse Android Development Tools (ADT) as the primary IDE for Android application development. Android Studio and the Software Development Kit can be downloaded directly from Google.

Features of Android Studio

Studio has following salient features for android application development:

- **Intelligent code editor:** Android Studio provides an intelligent code editor capable of advanced code completion, refactoring, and code analysis. The powerful code editor helps you be a more productive Android app developer.

- **Project Wizard:** New project wizards make it easier than ever to start a new project. Start projects using template code for patterns such as navigation drawer and view pagers, and even import Google code samples from GitHub.

- **Multi-screen app development:** Build apps for Android phones, tablets, Android Wear, Android TV, Android Auto and Google Glass. With the new Android ProjectView and module support in Android Studio, it's easier to manage app projects and resources.

- **Virtual devices for all shapes and sizes:** Android Studio comes pre-configured with an optimized emulator image. The updated and streamlined Virtual Device Manager provides pre-defined device profiles for common Android devices.

- **Android builds evolved, with Gradle:** Create multiple APKs for your Android app with different features using the same project.

To develop apps for Android, you use a set of tools that are included in Android Studio. In addition to using the tools from Android Studio, you can also access most of the SDK tools from the command line.

App Workflow

The basic steps for developing applications encompass four development phases, which include:

- **Environment Setup:** During this phase you install and set up your development environment. You also create Android Virtual Devices (AVDs) and connect hardware devices on which you can install your applications.
- **Project Setup and Development:** During this phase you set up and develop your Android Studio project and application modules, which contain all of the source code and resource files for your application.
- **Building, Debugging and Testing:** During this phase you build your project into a debuggable .apk package(s) that you can install and run on the emulator or an Android-powered device. Android Studio uses a build system based on Gradle that provides flexibility, customized build variants, dependency resolution, and much more. If you're using another IDE, you can build your project using Gradle and install it on a device using adb.

Next, with Android Studio you debug your application using the Android Debug Monitor and device log messages along with the IntelliJ IDEA intelligent coding features. You can also use a JDWP-compliant debugger along with the debugging and logging tools that are provided with the Android SDK. Last, you test your application using various Android SDK testing tools.

- **Publishing:** During this phase you configure and build your application for release and distribute your application to users.

Android Virtual Devices (AVD)

An Android Virtual Device (AVD) is an emulator configuration that lets you model an actual device by defining hardware and software options to be emulated by the Android Emulator.An AVD consists of:

A hardware profile: Defines the hardware features of the virtual device. For example, you can define whether the device has a camera, whether it uses a physical QWERTY keyboard or a dialing pad, how much memory it has, and so on.

A mapping to a system image: You can define what version of the Android platform will run on the virtual device. You can choose a version of the standard Android platform or the system image packaged with an SDK add-on.

Other options: You can specify the emulator skin you want to use with the AVD, which lets you control the screen dimensions, appearance, and so on. You can also specify the emulated SD card to use with the AVD.

A dedicated storage area on your development machine: the device's user data (installed applications, settings, and so on) and emulated SD card are stored in this area.

Android Emulator is used to run, debug and test the android application. If you don't have the real device, it can be the best way to run, debug and test the application. It uses an open source processor emulator technology called **QEMU**. In the given image, you can see the android emulator, it displays the output of the hello android example.

Figure-3a

The easiest way to create an AVD is to use the graphical AVD Manager. You can also start the AVD Manager from the command line by calling the android tool with the avd options, from the <sdk>/tools/ directory. You can also create AVDs on the command line by passing the android tool options. You can create as many AVDs as you need, based on the types of device you want to model. To thoroughly test your application, you should create an AVD for each general device configuration (for example, different screen sizes and platform versions) with which your application is compatible and test your application on each one. Keep these points in mind when you are selecting a system image target for your AVD:

- The API Level of the target is important, because your application will not be able to run on a system image whose API Level is less than that required by your application, as specified in the minSdkVersion attribute of the application's manifest file.
- You should create at least one AVD that uses a target whose API Level is greater than that required by your application, because it allows you to test the forward compatibility of your application. Forward compatibility testing ensures that, when users who have downloaded your application receive a system update, your application will continue to function normally.
- If your application declares a uses-library element in its manifest file, the application can only run on a system image in which that external library is present. If you want to run your application on an emulator, create an AVD that includes the required library. Usually, you must create such an AVD using an Add-on component for the AVD's platform.

56

Using Hardware Device to test Application

When building a mobile application, it's important that you always test your application on a real device before releasing it to users. You can use any Android-powered device as an environment for running, debugging, and testing your applications. The tools included in the SDK make it easy to install and run your application on the device each time you compile. You can install your application on the device directly from Android Studio or from the command line with ADB.

Android Studio IDE Components

Figure-3b: Android studio IDE

Project Tool Window

Figure-3c: Android studio IDE

The newly created project and references to associated files are listed in the Project tool window located on the left hand side of the main project window. The user interface design for our activity is stored in a file named activity_hello_world.xml which can be located using the Project tool window as shown below in Figure.

Double click on the file to load it into the User Interface Designer tool which will appear in the center panel of the Android Studio main window as shown below:

Component Tree Panel

Component Tree panel is by default located in the upper right hand corner of the Designer panel and is shown in figure and shows layout used for user interface.

Figure-3d: Component Tree Panel

Palette

On left hand side of the panel is a palette containing different categories of user interface components that may be used to construct a user interface, such as buttons, labels and text fields. Android supports a variety of different layouts that provide different levels of control over how visual user interface components are positioned and managed on the screen.

Designer Window

This is where you design your user interface. In the top of the Designer window is a menu set to Nexus 4/5 device which is shown in the Designer panel.

To change the orientation of the device representation between landscape and portrait simply use the drop down menu immediately to the right of the device selection menu showing the icon.

Figure-3e: Designer Window

Property Window

Property Window allows setting different properties of selected component.

Figure-3f: Property Window

XML Editing Panel

We can modify user interface by modifying the activity_hello_world.xml using UI Designer tool but we can also modify design by editing XML file also. At the bottom of the Designer panel are two tabs labeled Design and Text respectively. To switch to the XML view simply select the Text tab as shown in figure. At the right hand side of the XML editing panel is the Preview panel and shows the current visual state of the layout.

Figure-3g: XML Editing Panel

Previewing the Layout

In above figure, layout has been previewed of the Nexus 4/5 device. The layout can be tested for other devices by making selections from the device menu in the toolbar across the top edge of the Designer panel. We can also preview screen size for all currently configured device as shown in figure.

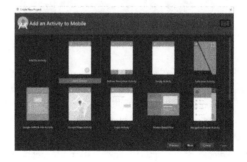

Figure-3i: Previewing the Layout

Android Studio Code Editor Customization

We customize code editor for font, displaying quick help when mouse moves over code.

Font Customization:

From File menu select settings option following dialog will open.

Select Colors & Fonts option. In scheme Default scheme is displayed. Click "Save As…" Button and give new name as "My Settings" to scheme. Now select font option as shown below and customize font as per your requirement.

Figure-3j

Show quick doc on mouse move

In android studio code editor, when you move your mouse over a method, class or interface, a documentation window would appear with a description of that programming element. This feature is by default disabled in android studio. This feature can be enabled in android studio as follows.

From file menu select settings option following dialog box appears. Select General option from list and scroll down to checkbox highlighted with red rectangle in below figure. Then press OK.

Best Practices

Action	Android Studio Key Command
Command look-up (autocomplete command name)	CTRL + SHIFT + A
Project quick fix	ALT + ENTER
Reformat code	CTRL + ALT + L (Win) OPTION + CMD + L (Mac)
Show docs for selected API	CTRL + Q (Win) F1 (Mac)
Show parameters for selected method	CTRL + P
Generate method	ALT + Insert (Win) CMD + N (Mac)
Jump to source	F4 (Win) CMD + down-arrow (Mac)
Delete line	CTRL + Y (Win) CMD + Backspace (Mac)
Search by symbol name	CTRL + ALT + SHIFT + N (Win) OPTION + CMD + O (Mac)

Table-3

Following table lists project and editor key commands:

Action	Android Studio Key Command
Build	CTRL + F9 (Win), CMD + F9 (Mac)
Build and run	SHIFT + F10 (Win), CTRL + R (Mac)
Toggle project visibility	ALT + 1 (Win), CMD + 1 (Mac)
Navigate open tabs	ALT + left-arrow; ALT + right-arrow (Win) CTRL + left-arrow; CTRL + right-arrow (Mac)

Table-4

You can change these shortcuts from file menu settings option as shown below.

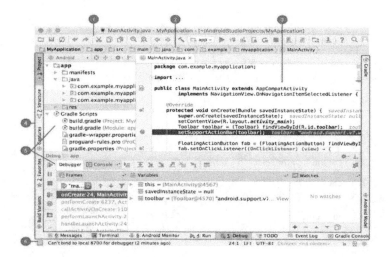

Figure-3k

1. The **toolbar** lets you carry out a wide range of actions, including running your app and launching Android tools.

2. The **navigation bar** helps you navigate through your project and open files for editing. It provides a more compact view of the structure visible in the **Project** window.

3. The **editor window** is where you create and modify code. Depending on the current file type, the editor can change. For example, when viewing a layout file, the editor displays the Layout Editor.

4. The **tool window bar** runs around the outside of the IDE window and contains the buttons that allow you to expand or collapse individual tool windows.

5. The **tool windows** give you access to specific tasks like project management, search, version control, and more. You can expand them and collapse them.

6. The **status bar** displays the status of your project and the IDE itself, as well as any warnings or messages.

Figure-3l

CHAPTER - 4
Building a Sample Android Application

So, without any further ado, let's dive straight in! Generally a program is defined in terms of functionality and data, and an Android application is not an exception. It performs processing, show information on the screen, and takes data from a variety of sources.

To Develop Android applications for mobile devices with resource constraint requires a systematic understanding of the application lifecycle. This CHAPTER introduces you with the most important components of Android applications and provides you with a more detailed understanding of how to create and run an Android application.

Building a sample Android application using Android Studio

Whether all of the required development packages are installed and functioning correctly. The simple way to realize this aim is to create an Android application and compile and run it. This topic will explain how to create a simple Android application project using Android Studio. Once the project has been created, a later CHAPTER will explore the use of the Android emulator environment to perform a test run of the application.

Creating a New Android Project

The first step in the application development process is to create a new project within the Android Studio environment. Launch Android Studio so that the "Welcome to Android Studio" screen appears as shown. This dialog box is used to start up a new Android Studio project, work with an existing project, and more. It can be accessed by selecting Android Studio from the Windows Start menu, or the equivalent on another platform.

To create the new project, simply click on the Start a new Android Studio project option to display the first screen of the New Project wizard as shown in figure

Figure-4a

In the New Project window, set the Application name field to HelloWorld. The application name is the name by which the application will be referenced and identified within Android Studio and is also the name that will be used when the completed application goes on sale in the Google Play store.

Figure-4b

The Package Name is used to uniquely identify the application within the Android application ecosystem. It should be based on the reversed URL of your domain name followed by the name of the application. For example, if your domain is ajitvoice.in, and the application has been named HelloWorld, then the package name might be specified as follows:
in.ajitvoice.HelloWorld

Make sure on that Phone and Tablet is the only box that is checked.
If you want to test the app on your own phone, make sure the minimum SDK should

be below your mobile's OS level.

Click on Next.

Figure-4c

Select Blank Activity from list of all activities.

Click on Next.

Leave all of the Activity name fields as it is.

Click on Finish.

Figure-4d

This will create project structure like this:

Figure-4e

Open Android Layout File (activity_main.xml)

The UI of our application will be designed in this file and it will contain Design and Text modes. It will exist in the layouts folder and the structure of activity_main.xml file in Design mode like as shown below.

We can make required design modifications in activity_main.xml file either using Design or Text modes. If we switch to Text mode activity_main.xml file will contain code like as shown below.

```
<?xml version="1.0" encoding="utf-8"?>
<android.support.constraint.ConstraintLayout
xmlns:android="http://schemas.android.com/apk/res/android"
   xmlns:app="http://schemas.android.com/apk/res-auto"
   xmlns:tools="http://schemas.android.com/tools"
   android:layout_width="match_parent"
   android:layout_height="match_parent"
   tools:context="in.ajitvoice.helloworld.MainActivity">
```

```
<TextView
    android:layout_width="wrap_content"
    android:layout_height="wrap_content"
    android:text="Hello World!"
    app:layout_constraintBottom_toBottomOf="parent"
    app:layout_constraintLeft_toLeftOf="parent"
    app:layout_constraintRight_toRightOf="parent"
    app:layout_constraintTop_toTopOf="parent" />
</android.support.constraint.ConstraintLayout>
```

Android Main Activity File (MainActivity.java)

The main activity file in android application is MainActivity.java and it will exists in java folder. The MainActivity.java file will contain the java code to handle all the activities related to our app.

Following is the default code of MainActivity.java file which is generated by our HelloWorld application.

```
package in.ajitvoice.helloworld;
import android.support.v7.app.AppCompatActivity;
import android.os.Bundle;
public class MainActivity extends AppCompatActivity
{
    @Override
    protected void onCreate(Bundle savedInstanceState)
{
        super.onCreate(savedInstanceState);
        setContentView(R.layout.activity_main);
}
}
```

Run the HelloWorld Application

Building your Android App

If you haven't already, start up Android Studio. The menu bar provides a Build menu, which you'll use to access Gradle and build the example application.

Select Make Project from the Build menu. You should observe a Gradle Build Running message on the status bar. After a little while, you should observe a Gradle Build Finished message. Click on this message and the Event Log window appears.

There's more than one way to build an Android app. For example, you could select Rebuild Project from the Build menu. Another approach is to actually run the app. If necessary, Gradle will automatically rebuild the app before its APK is installed and the app is run.

Do more with the Build menu

Android Studio's Build menu lets you perform several build tasks. For example, you could use the Generate Signed Bundle / APK menu item to build a signed app bundle or APK.

Running your Android app

In this section I'll show you how to run an Android application two ways: first on an emulated device, and then on an actual device. For my example I'll be using an Amazon Kindle Fire HD tablet, but the instructions should generally apply to the device of your choice.

Run your Android app on an emulated device
You can run the example application (W2A) or any other app by selecting Run 'app' in the Run menu. Alternatively, you can click the green triangle button on the toolbar. Either way, Android Studio responds with the Select Deployment Target dialog box.

- Press Shift+F10 or 'Run App' button in taskbar. It will launch following dialog box.
- Select Launch emulator option and select your Android virtual device and Press OK.
- The Android emulator starts up, which might take a moment.
- Press the Menu button to unlock the emulator.
- The application starts.
- Click the Home button in the Emulator to end the application.
- Pull up the Application Drawer to see installed applications.

Recall that earlier you created a few AVDs using the AVD Manager. So which one will be launched by Android Studio when you run an Android application? Android studio will check the target that you specified (when you created a new project), comparing it against the list of AVDs that you have created. The first one that matches will be launched to run your application.

If you have more than one suitable AVD running prior to debugging the application, Android Studio will display the Android Device Chooser window, which enables you to select the desired emulator/device to debug the application.

protected void onCreate(Bundle savedInstanceState)

What is Bundle?

Bundles are generally used for passing data between various Android activities. It depends on you what type of values you want to pass, but bundles can hold all types of values and pass them to the new activity. Bundles are generally used for passing data from one activity to another. Basically here concept of key-value pair is used where the data that one wants to pass is the value of the map, which can be later retrieved by using the key.

What is the savedInstanceState Bundle?

The savedInstanceState is a reference to a Bundle object that is passed into the onCreate method of every Android Activity. Activities have the ability, under special circumstances, to restore themselves to a previous state using the data stored in this bundle. If there is no available instance data, the savedInstanceState will be null. For example, the savedInstanceState will always be null the first time an Activity is started, but may be non-null if an Activity is destroyed during rotation.

When is the savedInstanceState useful?

There is one situation where using the savedInstanceState is almost mandatory: when the Activity gets destroyed during rotation. One way that Android handles rotation is to completely destroy and then re-create the current Activity. When the Activity is being destroyed, any state related information that is saved in onSaveInstanceState will be available when the Activity comes back online.

Another situation is when your Activity gets backgrounded. When an Activity is in a backgrounded state (either after onPause or onStop) it can be destroyed at any time with no notice. In the event that the OS kills your Activity without killing your Application, the OS will first save your outState Bundle so you can later return to your previous state.

What should be saved?

The savedInstanceState Bundle should only save information directly related to the current Activity state. Examples of this include:

1. User selections – A user selects a tab. In onSaveInstanceState the tab selection gets added to the outState Bundle. During the next onCreate, the selected tab will be available within the Bundle, and the Activity should default to having that tab selected.

2. Scroll view positions – A user scrolls half way through a ScrollView. The current position of the ScrollView should be saved in onSaveInstanceState then restored when the Activity is re-created.

3. User-submitted data – If a user writes their username into a text box, they would expect the username to still be present when the Activity is resumed.

What should not be saved?

In general (with few exceptions), the following kinds of data should never be saved into the Bundle:

- Files
- Database data
- Images
- Videos
- Anything downloaded from the web (feed data)
- Models (the data kind, not the people kind)

super.onCreate(savedInstanceState);

Why do we use super.onCreate(......)?

Every Activity you make is started through a sequence of method calls. onCreate() is the first of these calls. Each and every one of your Activities extends android.app.Activity either directly or by sub-classing another subclass of Activity.

In Java, when you inherit from a class, you can override its methods to run your own code in them. A very common example of this is the overriding of the toString() method when extending java.lang.Object.

71

When we override a method, we have the option of completely replacing the method in our class, or of extending the existing parent class' method. By calling super.onCreate(savedInstanceState);, you tell the Dalvik VM (Older Version) to run your code in addition to the existing code in the onCreate() of the parent class. If you leave out this line, then only your code is run. The existing code is ignored completely.

However, you must include this super call in your method, because if you don't then the onCreate() code in Activity is never run, and your app will run into all sorts of problem like having no Context assigned to the Activity (though you'll hit a SuperNotCalledException before you have a chance to figure out that you have no context).

In short, Android's own classes can be incredibly complex. The code in the framework classes handles stuff like UI drawing, house cleaning and maintaining the Activity and application life cycles. super calls allow developers to run this complex code behind the scenes, while still providing a good level of abstraction for our own apps.

setContentView(R.layout.activity_main);

This is a Java method called setContentView. It sets the XML file you want as your main layout when the app starts. In between round brackets, you need the name and location of your layout file. The letter R in the round brackets is short for res. This is the resource folder where those drawable, layout, mipmap, and values folders are. The layout.activity_main part points to the activity_main XML file, which is in the layout folder of res. If you wanted a different XML file to load when your app starts, you'd point to a different file:

setContentView(R.layout.some_other_xml_file);

The Project and Editor Windows

When you enter the main window, you observe the Project window showing only app and Gradle Scripts. You'll have to expand the app branch of the project tree to observe more details.

The Project window is organized into a tree whose main branches are app and Gradle Scripts. The app branch is further organized into manifests, java and res sub-branches:

- manifests stores AndroidManifest.xml, which is an XML file that describes the structure of an Android app. This file also records permission settings (where applicable) and other details about the app.
- java stores an app's Java source files according to a package hierarchy, which is ca.javajeff.w2a in this example. It also organizes files for testing purposes.
- res stores an app's resource files, which are organized into drawable, layout, mipmap, and values subbranches:
  - drawable is a mostly empty location in which to store an app's artwork; initially, the XML files for the launcher foreground and background adaptive icons are stored here.
  - layout is a location containing an app's layout files; main.xml (the main activity's layout file) is initially stored here.
  - mipmap is a location containing various ic_launcher.png files, which store launcher screen icons of different resolutions.
  - values is a location containing colors.xml, strings.xml, and styles.xml.

The Gradle Scripts branch identifies various .gradle (such as build.gradle) and .properties (such as local.properties) files that are used by Android Studio's Gradle-based build system.

Each branch/subbranch corresponds to a directory name or to a file name. For example, res corresponds to the res directory and strings.xml corresponds to the strings.xml file.

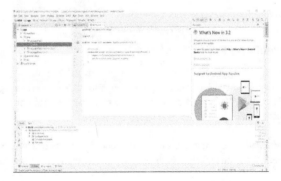

Figure-4f

Android Emulator

The Android emulator is an Android Virtual Device (AVD), which represents a specific Android device. We can use the Android emulator as a target device to execute and test our Android application on our PC. The Android emulator provides almost all the functionality of a real device. We can get the incoming phone calls and text messages. It also gives the location of the device and simulates different network speeds. Android emulator simulates rotation and other hardware sensors. It accesses the Google Play store, and much more.

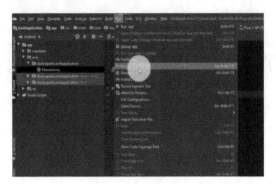

Figure-4g

Requirement and recommendations

The Android emulator takes additional requirements beyond the basic system requirement for Android Studio. These requirements are given below:

- SDK Tools 26.1.1 or higher
- 64-bit processor
- Windows: CPU with UG (unrestricted guest) support
- HAXM 6.2.1 or later (recommended HAXM 7.2.0 or later)

Install the emulator

The Android emulator is installed while installing the Android Studio. However some components of emulator may or may not be installed while installing Android Studio. To install the emulator component, select the Android Emulator component in the SDK Tools tab of the SDK Manager.

Running Apps on Your Device

When building an Android app, it's important that you always test your application on a real device in addition to emulators. This page describes how to set up your development environment and Android-powered device for testing and debugging on the device. If you want an ideal SIM-unlocked phone to test on, then you might consider a Pixel phone.

Connect your Phone to Computer

Plug in your device to your computer with a USB cable. If you're developing on Windows, you might need to install this universal ADB USB driver or find your specific USB driver for your device.

Enable USB Debugging

The next step is to enable USB debugging so your phone can interact with your computer in a developer mode. The following steps are needed:

- ★ (Windows Only) Install this ADB Driver
- ★ Plug-in your Android Device to Computer via USB
- ★ Open the "Settings" App on the Device
- ★ Scroll down to bottom to find "About phone" item
- ★ Scroll down to bottom to find "Build number" section
- ★ Tap on "Build Number" 7 times in quick succession
- ★ You should see the message "You are now a developer!"
- ★ Go back to main "Settings" page
- ★ Scroll down bottom to find "Developer options" item
- ★ Turn on "USB Debugging" switch and hit "OK"
- ★ Unplug and re-plug the device
- ★ Dialog appears "Allow USB Debugging?"
- ★ Check "Always allow from this computer" and then hit "OK"

Running your App

Now, we can launch apps from Android Studio onto our device:

* ★ Select one of your projects and click "Run" from the toolbar.
* ★ In the "Choose Device" window that appears, select the "Choose a running device" radio button, select the device, and click OK.

Once Gradle finishes building, Android Studio should install the app on your connected device and start it.

What's happening behind the scenes?

Finally you have run your first HelloWorld app on your emulator, Congratulations! But here are a few things that happened when you clicked the Play button.

* All your Java source code gets compiled into .class files by the Java compiler.
* All your .class files gets converted into a single .dex file by the dx tool, which is the part of Android SDK Tools.
* .dex file is a Dalvik Executable file that runs inside the Android Runtime(ART) when the app is launched.
* This .dex file is packaged with Android Manifest and other app resources files by Android Application Packaging Tool (aapt) to yield android package file, .apk
* Only a signed app can run on a device/emulator to ensure its authenticity, therefore the .apk file is signed using the jarsigner utility.
* zipalign utility is used to optimize the .apk file, and finally makes it ready for installation.

Gradle

Gradle is a build system, which is responsible for code compilation, testing, deployment and conversion of the code into .dex files and hence running the app on the device.

As Android Studio comes with Gradle system pre-installed, there is no need to install additional runtime softwares to build our project. Whenever you click on Run button in android studio, a gradle task automatically triggers and starts building the project and after gradle completes its task, app starts running in AVD or in the connected device.

A build system like Gradle is not a compiler, linker etc, but it controls and supervises the operation of compilation, linking of files, running test cases, and eventually bundling the code into an apk file for your Android Application.

There are two build.gradle files for every android studio project of which, one is for application and other is for project level(module level) build files.

Conversion of Android Code to APK with Gradle

In the build process, the compiler takes the source code, resources, external libraries JAR files and AndroidManifest.xml(which contains the meta-data about the application) and convert them into .dex(Dalvik Executable files) files, which includes bytecode. That bytecode is supported by all android devices to run your app. Then APK Manager combines the .dex files and all other resources into single apk file. APK Packager signs debug or release apk using respective debug or release keystore.

Debug apk is generally used for testing purpose or we can say that it is used at development stage only. When your app is complete with desired features and you are ready to publish your application for external use then you require a Release apk signed using a release keystore.
Now lets shed some light on the gradle files.

setting.gradle
The setting.gradle(Gradle setting) file is used to specify all the modules used in your app.

build.gradle (project level)
The Top level (module) build.gradle file is project level build file, which defines build configurations at project level. This file applies configurations to all the modules in android application project.

build.gradle (application level)
The Application level build.gradle file is located in each module of the android project. This file includes your package name as applicationID, version name(apk version), version code, minimum and target sdk for a specific application module. When you are including external libraries(not the jar files) then you need to mention it in the app level gradle file to include them in your project as dependencies of the application.

Android Typing Indicator App

We have seen Typing Indicators in various apps like Facebook, Instagram, Messenger, Twitter, etc. If we want to make a chat app then typing indicator is one of the features, we want in our app. it will help to achieve a better UI.

To learn its implementation, let's add an Android Typing Indicator in our android app.

Step 1: Create a new Project
Open Your Android Studio Click on "Start a new Android Studio project"(Learn how to set up Android Studio and create your first Android project)

Choose "Empty Activity" from the project template window and click on Next.

Enter the App Name, Package name, save location, language (Java/Kotlin, we will use Java for this tutorial), and the minimum SDK (we are using API 19: Android 4.4 (KitKat)).

Next click on the Finish button after filling in the above details.

Now, wait for the project to finish building.

Step 2: Adding the dependency
Go to Gradle Scripts -> build.gradle (Module: app) section and import below dependencies and click the "sync Now" show at the top.

```
dependencies
{
//Adding typing indicator
 implementation 'com.qifan.typingIndicator:typingIndicator:0.1.0'
}
```

Step 3: UI Part
Before applying any changes to the activity_main.xml file, we need a round rectangle image as typing indicator background, you can download any round rectangle images and put the image in the app -> res -> drawable, and give it a suitable name.

Now, go to app -> res -> layout -> activity_main.xml and add ChatTypingIndicatorView and change the background color of RelativeLayout to #2d2d2d as shown below.

```
<?xml version = "1.0" encoding = "utf-8"?>
<RelativeLayout xmlns:android="http://schemas.android.com/apk/res/android"
    xmlns:tools="http://schemas.android.com/tools"
    android:layout_width="match_parent"
```

```
    android:layout_height="match_parent"
    android:background="#2d2d2d"
    xmlns:app="http://schemas.android.com/apk/res-auto"
    tools:context=".MainActivity">
    <!– typing indicator -->
    <com.qifan.library.ChatTypingIndicatorView
        android:backgroundTint="#ffff"
        android:layout_centerInParent="true"
        android:gravity="center"
        android:id="@+id/oklIndicatorView"
        android:layout_width="160dp"
        android:layout_height="80dp"
        android:minHeight="40dp"
        android:padding="12dp"
        android:background="@drawable/round_rect"
        app:dotSize="12dp" />
</RelativeLayout>
```

Step 4: Coding Part

Open MainActivity.java file then create and initialize the ChatTypingIndicatorView object oklChatIndicatorView, and then call the startDotAnimation using the object. code of the MainActivity.java is shown below:

```
package in.ajitvoice.project;

import androidx.appcompat.app.AppCompatActivity;
import android.os.Bundle;
import com.qifan.library.ChatTypingIndicatorView;
public class MainActivity extends AppCompatActivity {

    ChatTypingIndicatorView oklChatIndicatorView;
    @Override
    protected void onCreate(Bundle savedInstanceState) {
        super.onCreate(savedInstanceState);
        setContentView(R.layout.activity_main);

        oklChatIndicatorView=(ChatTypingIndicatorView)findViewById(R.id.oklIndicatorView);
        oklChatIndicatorView.startDotAnimation();
    }
}
```

Output:
In the below snapshots, you can see how ChatTypingIndicatorView will look in the android application.

When App is opened for the first time:

Figure-4g

CHAPTER - 5
Android Project Structure and Basics

When you create a new Android project, you get several items in the project's root directory which is discussed in sub subsequent sections.

When you create an Android project as discussed in previous CHAPTER, you provide the fully -qualified class name of the "main" activity for the application (e.g.,in.ajitvoice.HelloWorld).

You will then find that your project's src/ tree already has the namespace directory tree in place, plus a stub Activity subclass representing your main activity (e.g., src/com/ajitvoice/HelloWorld.java). You can modify this file and add others to the src/tree as per requirement implement your application.

When you compile the project for first time, in the "main" activity's namespace directory, the Android build chain will create R.java. This contains a number of constants tied to the various resources you placed out in the res/directory tree. You should not modify R.java yourself, letting the Android tools handle it for you. You will see throughout many of the samples where we reference things in R.java (e.g., referring to a layout's identifier via R.layout.main).

Android Project Structure

An Android project contains everything that defines your Android app. The SDK tools require that your projects follow a specific structure so it can compile and package your application correctly. Android Studio takes care of all this for you.

A module is the first level of control within a project that encapsulates specific types of source code files and resources. There are several types of modules with a project:

When you use the Android development tools to create a new project and the module, the essential files and folders will be created for you. As your application grows in complexity, you might require new kinds of resources, directories, and files.

Module	Description
Android Application Modules	It contain source code, resource files, and application level settings, such as the module-level build file, resource files, and Android Manifest file.
Test Modules	It contains code to test your application projects and is built into test applications that run on a device.
Library Modules	It contains shareable Android source code and resources that you can reference in Android projects. This is useful when you have common code that you want to reuse.
App Engine Modules	They are App Engine java Servlet Module for backend development, App Engine java Endpoints Module to convert server -side Java code annotations into RESTful backend APIs, and App Engine Backend with Google Cloud Messaging to send push notifications from your server to your Android devices.

Table-4

Project Files

Android Studio project files and settings provide project wide settings that apply across all modules in the project.

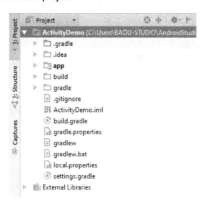

Figure-5a

File	Meaning
.idea	Directory for IntelliJ IDEA settings.
App	Application module directories and files.
Build	This directory stores the build output for all project modules.
Gradle	Contains the gradler-wrapper files.
.gitignore	Specifies the untracked files that Git should ignore.
build.gradle	Customizable properties for the build system.
gradle.properties	Project-wide Gradle settings.
gradlew	Gradle startup script for Unix.
gradlew.bat	Gradle startup script for Windows.
local.properties	Customizable computer-specific properties for the build system, such as the path to the SDK installation.
.iml	Module file created by the IntelliJ IDEA to store module information.
settings.gradle	Specifies the sub-projects to build.

Table-5

Android Application Modules

Android Application Modules contain things such as application source code and resource files. Most code and resource files are generated for you by default, while others should be created if required. The following directories and files comprise an Android application module:

Figure-5b

83

File	Meaning
build/	Contains build folders for the specified build variants. Stored in the main application module.
libs/	Contains private libraries. Stored in the main application module.
src/	Contains your stub Activity file, which is stored at src/main/java/<ActivityName>.java. All other source code files (such as .java or .aidl files) go here as well.
androidTest/	Contains the instrumentation tests.
main/jni/	Contains native code using the Java Native Interface (JNI).
main/gen/	Contains the Java files generated by Android Studio, such as your R.java file and interfaces created from AIDL files.
main/assets/	This is empty. You can use it to store raw asset files. For example, this is a good location for textures and game data. Files that you save here are compiled into an .apk file as-is, and the original filename is preserved. You can navigate this directory and read files as a stream of bytes using the AssetManager.
main/res/	Contains application resources, such as drawable files, layout files, and string values in the following directories.
anim/	For XML files that are compiled into animation objects.
color/	For XML files that describe colors.
drawable/	For bitmap files (PNG, JPEG, or GIF), 9-Patch image files, and XML files that describe Drawable shapes or Drawable objects that contain multiple states (normal, pressed, or focused).
mipmap/	For app launcher icons. The Android system retains the resources in this folder (and density-specific folders such as mipmap-xxxhdpi) regardless of the screen resolution of the device where your app is installed. This behavior allows launcher apps to pick the best resolution icon for your app to display on the home screen.
layout/	XML files that are compiled into screen layouts (or part of a screen).
menu/	For XML files that define application menus.

raw/	For arbitrary raw asset files. Saving asset files here is essentially the same as saving them in the assets/ directory. The only difference is how you access them. These files are processed by aapt and must be referenced from the application using a resource identifier in the R class. For example, this is a good place for media, such as MP3 or Ogg files.
values/	For XML files that define resources by XML element type. Unlike other resources in the res/ directory, resources written to XML files in this folder are not referenced by the file name. Instead, the XML element type controls how the resources defined within the XML files are placed into the R class.
xml/	For miscellaneous XML files that configure application components. For example, an XML file that defines a PreferenceScreen, AppWidgetProviderInfo, or Searchability Metadata.
AndroidManife st.xml	The control file that describes the nature of the application and each of its components. For instance, it describes: certain qualities about the activities, services, intent receivers, and content providers; what permissions are requested; what external libraries are needed; what device features are required, what API Levels are supported or required; and others.
.gitignore/	Specifies the untracked files ignored by git.
app.iml/	IntelliJ IDEA module
build.gradle	Customizable properties for the build system. You can edit this file to override default build settings used by the manifest file and also set the location of your keystore and key alias so that the build tools can sign your application when building in release mode. This file is integral to the project, so maintain it in a source revision control system.
proguard- rules.pro	ProGuard settings file.

Table-6

1

Folder Structure
Android Project view

In Project view, we can see lots of files and directories. The most important of which are the following :

project-name/
build/
This folder contains build outputs.

libs/
This folder contains private libraries.

src/
This folder contains all code and resource file.

src/androidTest/
This folder contains code for instrumentation tests that run on an Android device.

src/main/
This folder contains all our java source files. Also contains activity controllers, models, helpers, etc.

AndroidManifest.xml
This file describes the nature of the application and each of its components.

java/
This folder contains Java code sources.

gen/
This folder contains the Java files generated by Android Studio, such as your R.java file and interfaces created from AIDL files.

res/
This folder contains application resources, such as drawable files, layout files, and UI string.

assets/
This folder contains file that will be compiled into an .apk file.

test/
This folder contains code for tests.

build.gradle (module)
This describes module-specific build configurations.

build.gradle (project)
This represents your build configuration that apply to all modules.

Resources (res)

anim/
This folder contains XML files for animations required for an app. R.anim class is used to access these files.

color/
This folder contains XML files colors required for an app. R.color class is used to access these files.

drawable/
This folder contains Image files like .png, .jpg, .gif or XML files. R.drawable class is used to access them.

layout/
This folder contains XML files that represent UI layout. R.layout class is used to access them.

menu/
Application need menus such as Options menu, Context menu, Sub menu. This folder contains XML files that represent such type of menus. R.menu class is used to access them.

raw/
Some Arbitary files need to be saved in their raw form. So this folder is used to store them. Resources.openRawResource() with the resource ID, which is R.raw.filename is requred to open such files.

values/

This folder contains XML files that holds values such as colors, strings, and integers. For example :

arrays.xml : Holds array resources. R.array class is used to access them.

integers.xml : Holds integer resources. R.integer class is used to access them.

bools.xml : Holds boolean resources. R.bool class is used to access them.

colors.xml : Holds color values. R.color class is used to access them.

dimens.xml : Holds dimension values. R.dimen class is used to access them.

strings.xml : Holds string values. R.string class is used to access them.

styles.xml : Holds application styles. R.style class is used to access them.

xml/

Contains Arbitrary XML files. These files can be read at runtime by calling Resources.getXML(). Various settings/configuration can be saved here and used at run time.

Types of Modules

Android Studio offers a few distinct types of module:

Android app module: It provides a container for your app's source code, resource files, and app level settings such as the module-level build file and Android Manifest file. When you create a new project, the default module name is "app". In the Create New Module window, Android Studio offers the following types of app modules:

- Phone & Tablet Module

- Wear OS Module

- Android TV Module

- Glass Module

They each provide essential files and some code templates that are appropriate for the corresponding app or device type.

Dynamic feature module: It denotes a modularized feature of your app that can take advantage of Google Play's Dynamic Delivery. For example, with dynamic feature modules, you can provide your users with certain features of your app on-demand or as instant experiences through Google Play Instant.

Library module: It provides a container for your reusable code, which you can use as a dependency in other app modules or import into other projects. Structurally, a library module is the same as an app module, but when built, it creates a code archive file instead of an APK, so it can't be installed on a device.

In the Create New Module window, Android Studio offers the following library modules:

- **Android Library:** This type of library can hold all file types supported in an Android project, including source code, resources, and manifest files. The build result is an Android Archive file or AAR file that can be added as a dependency for your Android app modules.

- **Java Library:** This type of library can contain only Java source files. The build result is a Java Archive or JAR file that can be added as a dependency for your Android app modules or other Java projects.

Google Cloud module: it provides a container for your Google Cloud backend code. It has the required code and dependencies for a Java App Engine backend that uses HTTP, Cloud Endpoints, and Cloud Messaging to connect to your app. You can develop your backend to provide cloud services need by your app.

Project structure settings

To change various settings for your Android Studio project, open the project structure dialog by clicking File -> Project Structure. It contains the following sections:

- **SDK Location:** Sets the location of the JDK, Android SDK, and Android NDK that your project uses.
- **Project:** Sets the version for Gradle and the Android plugin for Gradle, and the repository location name.
- **Developer Services:** Contains settings for Android Studio add-in components from Google or other third parties.
- **Modules:** Allows you to edit module-specific build configurations, including the target and minimum SDK, the app signature, and library dependencies.

Anatomy of an Android Application

To Develop Android applications for mobile devices with resource constraint requires a systematic understanding of the application lifecycle. Important terminology for application building blocks terms are Context, Activity, and Intent. This section introduces you with the most important components of Android applications and provides you with a more detailed understanding of how Android applications function and interact with one another.

Important Android Terminology

Followings are the important terminology used in Android application development.

- **Context:** The context is the essential command for an Android application. It stores the current state of the application/object and all application related functionality can be accessed through the context. Typically you call it to get information regarding another part of your program such as an activity, package, and application.

- **Activity:** It is core to any Android application. An Android application is a collection of tasks, each of which is called an Activity. Each Activity within an application has an exclusive task or purpose. Typically, applications have one or more activities, and the main objective of an activity is to interact with the user.

- **Intent:** Intent is a messaging object which can be used to request an action from another app component. Each request is packaged as Intent. You can think of each such request as a message stating intent to do something. Intent mainly used for three tasks 1) to start an activity, 2) to start a service and 3) to deliver a broadcast.

- **Service:** Tasks that do not require user interaction can be encapsulated in a service. A service is most useful when the operations are lengthy (offloading time-consuming processing) or need to be done regularly (such as checking a server for new mail).

Basic Android API Packages

Application program interface (API) is a set of routines, protocols, and tools for building software applications. An API specifies how software components should interact and APIs are used when programming graphical user interface (GUI) components. Android offers a number of APIs for developing your applications. The following list of core APIs should provide an insight into what's available; all Android devices will offer support for at least these APIs:

API Package	Use
android.util	Provides common utility methods such as date/time manipulation, base64 encoders and decoders, string and number conversion methods, and XML utilities.
android.os	Provides basic operating system services, message passing, and inter-process communication on the device.
android.graphics	Provides low level graphics tools such as canvases, color filters, points, and rectangles that let you handle drawing to the screen directly.
android.text	Provides classes used to render or track text and text spans on the screen.
android.database	Contains classes to explore data returned through a content provider.
android.content	Contains classes for accessing and publishing data on a device.
android.view	Provides classes that expose basic user interface classes that handle screen layout and interaction with the user.
android.widget	The widget package contains (mostly visual) UI elements to use on your Application screen.
android.app	Contains high-level classes encapsulating the overall Android application model.
android.provider	Provides convenience classes to access the content providers supplied by Android.
android.webkit	Provides tools for browsing the web.

Table-7

Advanced Android API Packages

The core libraries provide all the functionality you need to start creating applications for Android,but it won't be long before you're ready to delve into the advanced APIs that offer the really exciting functionality.

Android hopes to target a wide range of mobile hardware, so be aware that the suitability and implementation of the following APIs will vary depending on the device upon which they are implemented.

API Package	Use
android.location	Contains the framework API classes that define Android location-based and related services.
android.media	Provides classes that manage various media interfaces in audio and video.
android.opengl	Provides an OpenGL ES static interface and utilities.
android.hardware	Provides support for hardware features, such as the camera and other sensors.
android.bluetooth	Provides classes that manage Bluetooth functionality, such as scanning for devices, connecting with devices, and managing data transfer between devices. The Bluetooth API supports both "Classic Bluetooth" and Bluetooth Low Energy.
android.net.wifi	Provides classes to manage Wi-Fi functionality on the device.
android.telephony	Provides APIs for monitoring the basic phone information, such as the network type and connection state, plus utilities for manipulating phone number strings.

Table-8

CHAPTER - 6
Android Manifest File

The manifest file declares the following:

- The app's package name.
- The components of the app such as activities, services, broadcast receivers, and content providers.
- Which device configurations it can handle.
- Intent filters that describe how the component can be started.
- Permissions required by the app.
- The hardware and software features the app requires.

Android Studio generally builds the manifest file for you when you create a project. For a simple application with a single activity and nothing else, the auto-generated manifest will work fine with little or no modifications.

Component of Manifest file

This topic describes some of the most important characteristics of your app which is stored in the manifest file.

name and application ID

The manifest file's root element requires an attribute for your app's package name, For example, the following snippet shows the root <manifest> element with the package name "in.ajitvoice.databasedemo":

```
<? xml version="1.0" encoding="utf-8"?>
<manifest xmlns:android="http://schemas.android.com/apk/res/android"
package="in.ajitvoice.databasedemo"
android:versionCode="1" android:versionName="1.0" >
...
</manifest>
```

While building your app into the final APK, the Android build tools use the package attribute for two things:

It applies this name as the namespace for your app's generated R.java class. With the above manifest, the R class is created at in.ajitvoice.databasedemo.R.

Android manifest file uses package this name to resolve any relative class names that are declared in the manifest file.

If, an activity declared as <activity android:name=".MainActivity"> is resolved to be in.ajitvoice.databasedemo.MainActivity.

You should keep in mind that once the APK is compiled, the package attribute also represents your app's universally unique application ID. After the build tools perform the above tasks based on the package name, they replace the package value with the value given to the applicationId property in your project's build.gradle file.

Components

For each app component that you create in your app, you must declare a corresponding XML element in the manifest file so that the system can start it.

- Foreach subclass of Activity, we have <activity>
- Foreach subclass of Service, we have <service>
- Foreach subclass of BroadcastReceiver we have <receiver>.
- For each subclass of ContentProvider, we have <provider>

The name of your subclass must be specified with the name attribute, using the full package designation,e.g. an Activity subclass can be declared as follows
<manifest package="in.ajitvoice.databasedemo" ... >

```
<application ... >
<activity android:name=".SQLiteDBActivity" ... >
...
</activity>
</application>
</manifest>
```

In above example, the activity name is resolved to
"in.ajitvoice.databasedemo.SQLiteDBActivity"

App activities, services, and broadcast receivers are activated by intents. It is an asynchronous messaging mechanism to match task requests with the appropriate Activity.

When an app issues intent to the system, the system locates an app component that can handle the intent based on intent filter declarations in each app's manifest file. The system launches an instance of the matching component and passes the Intent object to that component. If more than one app can handle the intent, then the user can select which app to use. An intent filters is defined with the <intent-filter> element as shown below;

```
<activity android:name=".SQLiteDBActivity">
<intent-filter>
<action android:name="android.intent.action.MAIN" />
<category android:name="android.intent.category.LAUNCHER" />
</intent-filter>
</activity>
```

A number of manifest elements have icon and label attributes for displaying a small icon and a text label, respectively, to users for the corresponding app component.

For example, the icon and label that are set in the <application> element are the default icon and label for each of the app's components.

The icon and label that are set in a component's <intent-filter> are shown to the user whenever that component is presented as an option to fulfill intent.

Permissions

Android apps must request permission to access personnel user data such as contacts, SMS, camera, files, internet etc. Each permission is identified by a unique label. For example, an app that needs to send and receive SMS messages must have the following line in the manifest:

```
<manifest ... >
<uses-permission android:name="android.permission.SEND_SMS" />
<uses-permission android:name="android.permission.RECEIVE_SMS" />
...
</manifest>
```

From API level 23, the user can approve or reject some app permissions at runtime. You must declare all permission requests with a <uses-permission> element in the manifest. If the permission is granted, the app is able to use the protected features. If not, its attempts to access those features fail.A new permission is declared with the <permission> element.

Device Compatibility

In manifest file is you can declare what types of hardware or software features your app requires and types of devices with which your app is compatible. It can't be installed on devices that don't provide the features or system version that your app requires.The following table shows the most common tags for specifying device compatibility.

Tag	Description
<uses-feature>	It allows you to declare hardware and software features your app needs
	Example
	<manifest ... >
	<uses-feature android:name="android.hardware.sensor.compass" android:required="true" />
	...
	</manifest>
<uses-sdk>	It indicates the minimum version with which your app is compatible element are overridden by corresponding properties in the build.gradle file.
	<manifest>
	<uses-sdkandroid:minSdkVersion="5" />
	...
	</manifest>

Table-9

3

File Conventions

Following are the conventions and rules that generally apply to all elements and attributes in the manifest file.

- Only the <manifest> and <application> elements are required. They each must occur only once, other elements can occur zero or more times.

- Elements at the same level are generally not ordered hence elements can be placed in any order.

- All attributes are optional but attributes must be specified so that an element can serve its purpose. If attributes are not provided then it indicates the default value.

- Except for some attributes of the root <manifest> element, all attribute names begin with an android: prefix.

Manifest elements reference

The following table provides links to reference documents for all valid elements in the AndroidManifest.xml file.

Element	Description
<action>	It is used to add an action to an intent filter.
<activity>	It is used to declare an activity component.
<activity-alias>	It is used to declare an alias for an activity.
<application>	It is used to declare the application.
<category>	It is used to add category name to an intent filter.
<compatible-screens>	It is used to specifies each screen configuration with which the application is compatible.
<data>	Adds a data specification to an intent filter.
<grant-uri-permission>	Specifies the subsets of app data that the parent content provider has permission to access.
<instrumentation>	Declares an Instrumentation class that enables you to monitor an application's interaction with the system.

<intent-filter>	Specifies the types of intents that an activity, service, or broadcast receiver can respond to.
<manifest>	The root element of the AndroidManifest.xml file.
<meta-data>	A name-value pair for an item of additional, arbitrary data that can be supplied to the parent component.
<path-permission>	Defines the path and required permissions for a specific subset of data within a content provider.
<permission>	Declares a security permission that can be used to limit access to specific components or features of this or other applications.
<permission-group>	Declares a name for a logical grouping of related permissions.
<permission-tree>	Declares the base name for a tree of permissions.
<provider>	Declares a content provider component.
<receiver>	Declares a broadcast receiver component.
<service>	Declares a service component.
<supports-gl-texture>	Declares a single GL texture compression format that the app supports.
<supports-screens>	Declares the screen sizes your app supports and enables screen compatibility mode for screens larger than what your app supports.
<uses-configuration>	Indicates specific input features the application requires.
<uses-feature>	Declares a single hardware or software feature that is used by the application.
<uses-library>	Specifies a shared library that the application must be linked against.
<uses-permission>	Specifies a system permission that the user must grant in order for the app to operate correctly.
<uses-sdk>	Lets you express an application's compatibility with one or more versions of the Android platform, by means of an API level integer.

Table-10

5

Example of Manifest file

The XML below is a simple example AndroidManifest.xml that declares two activities for the app.

```xml
<?xml version="1.0" encoding="utf-8"?>
<manifest xmlns:android="http://schemas.android.com/apk/res/android"
              package="in.ajitvoice.listnameactivity"
            android:versionCode="1" android:versionName="1.0" >
<uses-sdk android:minSdkVersion="8" android:targetSdkVersion="22" />
<application
android:allowBackup="true" android:icon="@mipmap/ic_launcher"
android:label="@string/app_name" android:theme="@style/AppTheme" >
<activity android:name="in.ajitvoice.listnameactivity.NameDisplayActivity"
android:label="@string/app_name" >
<intent-filter>
<action android:name="android.intent.action.MAIN" />
<category android:name="android.intent.category.LAUNCHER" />
</intent-filter>
</activity>
<activity
android:name="in.ajitvoice.listnameactivity.MultipleChoiceActivity"
android:label="@string/title_activity_multiple_choice" >
</activity>
</application>
</manifest>
```

CHAPTER - 7

Working with Activities

To Develop Android applications for mobile devices with resource constraint requires a systematic understanding of the application lifecycle. Important terminology for application building blocks terms are Context, Activity, and Intent. This CHAPTER introduces you with the most important components of Android applications and provides you with a more detailed understanding of how Android applications function and interact with one another.

The Activity class is a crucial component of an Android app, and the way activities are launched and put together is a fundamental part of the platform's application model. Unlike programming paradigms in which apps are launched with a main() method, the Android system initiates code in an Activity instance by invoking specific callback methods that correspond to specific stages of its lifecycle.

This CHAPTER introduces the concept of activities, and then provides some lightweight guidance about how to work with them.

What is Activity?

Mobile-app experience differs from its desktop counter part in that a user's interaction with the app doesn't always begin in the same place. Instead, the user journey often begins non-deterministically. For instance, if you open an email app from your home screen, you might see a list of emails. By contrast, if you are using a social media app that then launches your email app, you might go directly to the email app's screen for composing an email.

The Activity class is designed to facilitate this paradigm. When one app invokes another, the calling app invokes an activity in the other app, rather than the app as an atomic whole. In this way, the activity serves as the entry point for an app's interaction with the user. You implement an activity as a subclass of the Activity class.

An activity provides the window in which the app draws its UI. This window typically fills the screen, but may be smaller than the screen and float on top of other windows. Generally, one activity implements one screen in an app. For instance, one of an app's activities may implement a Preferences screen, while another activity implements a Select Photo screen.

Most apps contain multiple screens, which means they comprise multiple activities. Typically, one activity in an app is specified as the main activity, which is the first screen to appear when the user launches the app. Each activity can then start another activity in order to perform different actions. For example, the main activity in a simple e-mail app may provide the screen that shows an e-mail inbox. From there, the main activity might launch other activities that provide screens for tasks like writing e-mails and opening individual e-mails.

Although activities work together to form a cohesive user experience in an app, each activity is only loosely bound to the other activities; there are usually minimal dependencies among the activities in an app. In fact, activities often start up activities belonging to other apps. For example, a browser app might launch the Share activity of a social-media app. To use activities in your app, you must register information about them in the app's manifest, and you must manage activity life cycles appropriately. The rest of this document introduces these subjects.

The AndroidManifest.xml

For your app to be able to use activities, you must declare the activities, and certain of their attributes, in the manifest.
Declare activities: To declare your activity, open your manifest file and add an <activity> element as a child of the <application> element.

For example:
```
<manifest ... >
<application ... >
<activity android:name=".ExampleActivity" />

...
</application ... >

...
</manifest >
```

The only required attribute for this element is android:name, which specifies the class name of the activity. You can also add attributes that define activity characteristics such as label, icon, or UI theme.

Declare intent filters: Intent filters are a very powerful feature of the Android platform. They provide the ability to launch an activity based not only on an explicit request, but also an implicit one. For example, an explicit request might tell the system to "Start the Send Email activity in the Gmail app". By contrast, an implicit request tells the system to "Start a Send Email screen in any activity that can do the job". When the system UI asks a user which app to use in performing a task, that's an intent filter at work.

You can take advantage of this feature by declaring an <intent-filter> attribute in the <activity> element. The definition of this element includes an <action> element and, optionally, a <category> element and/or a <data> element. These elements combine to specify the type of intent to which your activity can respond. For example, the following code snippet shows how to configure an activity that sends text data, and receives requests from other activities to do so:

```
<activity android:name=".ExampleActivity" android:icon="@drawable/app_icon">
<intent-filter>
<action android:name="android.intent.action.SEND" />
<category android:name="android.intent.category.DEFAULT" />
<data android:mimeType="text/plain" />
</intent-filter>
</activity>
```

In this example, the <action> element specifies that this activity sends data. Declaring the <category> element as DEFAULT enables the activity to receive launch requests. The <data> element specifies the type of data that this activity can send. The following code snippet shows how to call the activity described above

```
// Create the text message with a string
Intent sendIntent = new Intent();
sendIntent.setAction(Intent.ACTION_SEND);
sendIntent.setType("text/plain");
sendIntent.putExtra(Intent.EXTRA_TEXT, textMessage);
// Start the activity
startActivity(sendIntent);
```

If you intend for your app to be self-contained and not allow other apps to activate its activities, you don't need any other intent filters. Activities that you don't want to make available to other applications should have no intent filters, and you can start them yourself using explicit intents.

Declare permissions: You can use the manifest's <activity> tag to control which apps can start a particular activity. A parent activity cannot launch a child activity unless both activities have the same permissions in their manifest. If you declare a <uses-permission> element for a particular activity, the calling activity must have a matching <uses-permission> element.

For example, if your app wants to use a hypothetical app named SocialApp to share a post on social media, SocialApp itself must define the permission that an app calling it must have:

```
<manifest>
<activity android:name="     "
        android:permission="com.google.socialapp.permission.SHARE_POST"
/>
```

Then, to be allowed to call SocialApp, your app must match the permission set in SocialApp's manifest:

```
<manifest>
<uses-permission android:name="com.google.socialapp.permission.SHARE_POST"/>
</manifest>
```

Life Cycle of an Activity

The Activity class is an important for application's whole lifecycle. Android applications can be multi-process, and the multiple applications to run concurrently if memory and processing power is available. Applications can have background processes, and applications can be interrupted/paused when events such as message or phone calls occur. There can be only one active application visible to the user at a time or in other words only a single Activity is in the foreground at any given time. Activities in the Android operating system are managed using an activity stack. When a new activity is started, it is placed on the top of the stack and becomes the running/foreground activity the previous activity always remains below it in the stack, and will not come to the foreground again until the new activity exits.

Activity States

An activity has essentially four states:

State	Description
Active or running	When an activity is in the foreground of the screen (at the top of the stack).
Paused	If an activity has lost focus but is still visible, it is paused. A paused activity maintains all state and member information and remains attached to the window manager, but can be killed by the system in extreme low memory situations.
Stopped	If an activity is completely hidden by another activity, it is stopped. It still retains all state and member information, it will often be killed by the system when memory is needed elsewhere.
Destroyed	If an activity is paused or stopped, the system can drop the activity from memory by either asking it to finish, or simply killing its process. When it is displayed again to the user, it must be completely restarted and restored to its previous state.

Table-11

Activity Events

The Activity base class defines a series of events that governs the life cycle of an activity. The Activity class defines the following events:

Event	Description
onCreate()	Called when the activity is first created
onStart()	Called when the activity becomes visible to the user
onResume()	Called when the activity starts interacting with the user
onStop()	Called when the activity is no longer visible to the user
onRestart()	Called when the activity has been stopped and is restarting again
onDestroy()	Called before the activity is destroyed by the system
onPause()	Called when the current activity is being paused and the previous activity is being resumed

Table-12

By default, the activity created for you contains the onCreate() event. Within this event handler is the code that helps to display the UI elements of your screen.

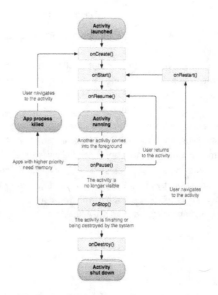

Figure-7a: important state paths of an Activity

The above figure shows the important state paths of an Activity. The square rectangles represent callback methods you can implement to perform operations when the Activity moves between states. The colored ovals are major states the Activity can be in.

Life Cycle of an Activity

The best way to understand the various stages experienced by an activity is to create a new project, .implement the various events, and then subject the activity to various user interactions.

1. Create a New Android Studio Project with project name ActivityDemo and Main Activity name as MainActivity.
2. In the MainActivity.java file, add the following statements in bold:

```
package in.ajitvoice.activitydemo;
import android.util.Log;
public class MainActivity extends ActionBarActivity
{ @Override
protected void onCreate(Bundle savedInstanceState)
{
super.onCreate(savedInstanceState);
setContentView(R.layout.activity_main); Log.d("Event", "In the onCreate() event");
}
    public void onStart()
{
    super.onStart(); Log.d("Event", "In the onStart() event");
}
    public void onRestart()
{
    super.onRestart(); Log.d("Event", "In the onRestart() event");
}
    public void onResume()
{
    super.onResume(); Log.d("Event", "In the onResume() event");
}
    public void onPause()
{
    super.onPause(); Log.d("Event", "In the onPause() event");
}
    public void onStop()
{
    super.onStop(); Log.d("Event", "In the onStop() event");
}
    public void onDestroy()
{
    super.onDestroy(); Log.d("Event", "In the onDestroy() event");
}}
```

3. Press Shift+F10 or
4. Run App button in taskbar. It will launch following dialog box. Press OK.

Figure-7b

5. When the activity is first loaded, you should see the following in the LogCat window.

6. Now press the back button on the Android Emulator, observe that the following is printed:

Figure-7c

7. Click the Home button and hold it there. Click the ActivityDemo icon and observe the following:

Figure-7d

8. On Android Emulator from notification area open settings on so that the activity is pushed to the background. Observe the output in the LogCat window:

Figure-7e

9. Notice that the onDestroy() event is not called, indicating that the activity is still in memory. Exit the settings by pressing the Back button. The activity is now visible again. Observe the output in the LogCat window:

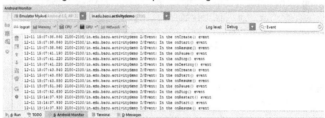

Figure-7f

Please note that the onRestart() event is now fired, followed by the onStart() and onResume() events.

This application uses logging feature of Android. To add logging support to ActivityDemo app, edit the file MainActivity.java to add the following import statement for the Log class:

import android.util.Log;

Logging is a valuable resource for debugging and learning Android. Android logging features are in the Log class of the android.util package. Some helpful methods in the android.util.Log class are shown in Table. We have used Log.d() method to print message in LogCat Window when particular event of activity fired.

15

Method	Purpose
Log.e()	Log errors
Log.w()	Log warnings
Log.i()	Log information messages
Log.d()	Log debug messages
Log.v()	Log verbose messages

Table-13

How to Send Data From One Activity to Second Activity in Android?

This article aims to tell and show how to "Send the data from one activity to second activity using Intent". In this example, we have two activities, activity_first which is the source activity, and activity_second which is the destination activity. We can send the data using the putExtra() method from one activity and get the data from the second activity using the getStringExtra() method.

In this example, one EditText is used to input the text. This text is sent to the second activity when the "Send" button is clicked. For this, Intent will start and the following methods will run:

putExtra() method is used for sending the data, data in key-value pair key is variable name and value can be Int, String, Float, etc.

getStringExtra() method is for getting the data(key) that is sent by the above method. according the data type of value there are other methods like getIntExtra(), getFloatExtra()

Step 1: Create a new project in Android Studio

To create a new project in Android Studio please refer to How to Create/Start a New Project in Android Studio. The code for that has been given in Java Programming Language for Android. This will create an XML file and a Java File. Please refer the pre-requisites to learn more about this step.

Figure-7g

Step 2: Working with the XML Files

Next, go to the activity_main.xml file, which represents the UI of the project. Below is the code for the activity_main.xml file. Comments are added inside the code to understand the code in more detail. Open the "activity_first_activity.xml" file and add the following widgets in a Relative Layout.
An EditText to Input the message
A Button to send the data

Also, Assign the ID to each component along with other attributes as shown in the image and the code below. The assigned ID on a component helps that component to be easily found and used in the Java files.
Syntax:
android:id="@+id/id_name"
Here the given IDs are as follows:

Send Button: send_button_id
input EditText: send_text_id

```
<?xml version="1.0" encoding="utf-8"?>
<RelativeLayout xmlns:android="http://schemas.android.com/apk/res/android"
    xmlns:tools="http://schemas.android.com/tools"
    android:layout_width="match_parent"
    android:layout_height="match_parent"
    tools:context=".first_activity">
```

```
<EditText
    android:id="@+id/send_text_id"
    android:layout_width="300dp"
    android:layout_height="wrap_content"
    android:layout_marginLeft="40dp"
    android:layout_marginTop="20dp"
    android:hint="Input"
    android:textSize="25dp"
    android:textStyle="bold" />

<Button
    android:id="@+id/send_button_id"
    android:layout_width="wrap_content"
    android:layout_height="40dp"
    android:layout_marginLeft="150dp"
    android:layout_marginTop="150dp"
    android:text="send"
    android:textStyle="bold" />
</RelativeLayout>
```

Figure-7h

Step 3: Working with the MainActivity File

Go to the MainActivity File and refer to the following code. Below is the code for the MainActivity File. Comments are added inside the code to understand the code in more detail. Now, after the UI, this step will create the Backend of the App. For this,

18

open the "first_activity" file and instantiate the components made in the XML file (EditText, send Button) using findViewById() method. This method binds the created object to the UI Components with the help of the assigned ID.
Syntax:

ComponentType object = (ComponentType)findViewById(R.id.IdOfTheComponent);
Syntax: for components used is as follows:
Button send_button= findViewById(R.id.send_button_id);
send_text = findViewById(R.id.send_text_id);

Setting up the Operations for the Sending and Receiving of Data. These Operations are as follows:

Add the listener to the send button and this button will send the data.
This is done as follows:
send_button.setOnClickListener(v -> {}
after clicking this button following operation will be performed.

Now create the String type variable to store the value of EditText which is input by the user. Get the value and convert it to string.
This is done as follows:
String str = send_text.getText().toString();

Now create the Intent object First_activity.java class to Second_activity class.
This is done as follows:
Intent intent = new Intent(getApplicationContext(), Second_activity.class);
where getApplicationContext() will fetch the current activity.

Put the value in the putExtra method in the key-value pair then start the activity.
This is done as follows:
intent.putExtra("message_key", str); startActivity(intent);
where "str" is the string value and the key is "message_key" this key will use to get the str value

Java Code
```
import android.content.Intent;
import android.os.Bundle;
import android.widget.Button;
import android.widget.EditText;
```

```
import androidx.appcompat.app.AppCompatActivity;
public class first_activity extends AppCompatActivity {

    // define the variable
    Button send_button;
    EditText send_text;

    @Override
    protected void onCreate(Bundle savedInstanceState) {
        super.onCreate(savedInstanceState);
        setContentView(R.layout.activity_first_activity);

        send_button = findViewById(R.id.send_button_id);
        send_text = findViewById(R.id.send_text_id);

        // add the OnClickListener in sender button after clicked this button following
        // Instruction will run
        send_button.setOnClickListener(v -> {
            // get the value which input by user in EditText and convert it to string
            String str = send_text.getText().toString();
            // Create the Intent object of this class Context() to Second_activity class
            Intent intent = new Intent(getApplicationContext(), Second_activity.class);
            // now by putExtra method put the value in key, value pair key is
            // message_key by this key we will receive the value, and put the string
            intent.putExtra("message_key", str);
            // start the Intent
            startActivity(intent);
        });
    }
}
```

Step 4: Creating Second_Activity to Receive the Data.

The steps to create the second activity are as follows:
android project > File > new > Activity > Empty Activity

Figure-7i

Step 5: Working with the Second XML File

Add TextView to display the received messages. assign an ID to Textview.

XML
```xml
<?xml version="1.0" encoding="utf-8"?>
<RelativeLayout xmlns:android="http://schemas.android.com/apk/res/android"
    xmlns:tools="http://schemas.android.com/tools"
    android:layout_width="match_parent"
    android:layout_height="match_parent"
    tools:context="i n.ajitvoice.ajitsingh.sendthedata.Second_activity">

    <TextView
        android:id="@+id/received_value_id"
        android:layout_width="300dp"
        android:layout_height="50dp"
        android:layout_marginLeft="40dp"
        android:layout_marginTop="20dp"
        android:textSize="40sp"
        android:textStyle="bold"
        android:layout_marginStart="40dp" />
</RelativeLayout>
```
The Second Activity is shown below:

21

Figure-7j

Step 6: Working with the SecondActivity File
Define the TextView variable, use findViewById() to get the TextView as shown above.
receiver_msg = (TextView) findViewById(R.id.received_value_id);

Now In the second_activity.java file create the object of getIntent to receive the value
in String type variable by the getStringExtra method using message_key.
Intent intent = getIntent();
String str = intent.getStringExtra("message_key");

The received value set in the TextView object of the second activity XML file
receiver_msg.setText(str);

Java
import android.content.Intent;
import android.os.Bundle;
import android.widget.TextView;
import androidx.appcompat.app.AppCompatActivity;

public class Second_activity extends AppCompatActivity {

    TextView receiver_msg;

22

```
@Override
protected void onCreate(Bundle savedInstanceState) {
    super.onCreate(savedInstanceState);
    setContentView(R.layout.activity_second_activity);

    receiver_msg = findViewById(R.id.received_value_id);
    // create the get Intent object
    Intent intent = getIntent();
    // receive the value by getStringExtra() method and
    // key must be same which is send by first activity
    String str = intent.getStringExtra("message_key");
    // display the string into textView
    receiver_msg.setText(str);
  }
}
```

How to set my Activity as main activity in android?

In AndroidManifest.xml file inside application tag add an activity tag and remove action MAIN from old activity tag set that as default.

```
<application...... >
  <activity
    android:name=".DefaultActivity"
    android:label="@string/app_name" >
    <intent-filter>
      <action android:name="android.intent.action.DEFAULT" />
    </intent-filter>
  </activity>
  <activity
    android:name=".NewActivity"
    android:label="@string/app_name" >
    <intent-filter>
      <action android:name="android.intent.action.MAIN" />

      <category android:name="android.intent.category.LAUNCHER" />
    </intent-filter>
  </activity>
</application>
```

ACTION_MAIN activity: Start up as the initial activity of a task, with no data input and no returned output.

CATEGORY_LAUNCHER: The activity can be the initial activity of a task and is listed in the top-level application launcher`.
It is very important:

```
<intent-filter>
   <action android:name="android.intent.action.MAIN" />
   <category android:name="android.intent.category.LAUNCHER" />
</intent-filter>
```

Context

As the name suggests, it is the context of current state of the application/object. It lets newly created objects understand what has been going on. Typically you call it to get information regarding other part of your program (activity, package/application). The application Context is the central location for all top-level application functionality. The Context class can be used to manage application specific configuration details as well as application-wide operations and data. Use the application Context to access settings and resources shared across multiple Activity instances.

Retrieving the Application Context

You can get the context by invoking **getApplicationContext()**, **getContext()**, **getBaseContext()** or this (when in the activity class). You can retrieve the Context for the current process using the getApplicationContext() method, like this:

Context context = getApplicationContext();

Uses of the Application Context

After you have retrieved a valid application Context, it can be used to access application-wide features and services. Typical uses of context are:

Creating new views, adapters, listeners object

```
TextView tv = new TextView(getContext());

ListAdapter adapter = new SimpleCursorAdapter(getApplicationContext(), ...);
```

Retrieving Application Resources: You can retrieve application resources using the getResources() method of the application Context. The most straightforward way to retrieve a resource is by using its resource identifier, a unique number automatically generated within the R.java class. The following example retrieves a String instance from the application resources by its resource ID:

```
String greeting = getResources().getString(R.string.settings);
```

Retrieving Shared Application Preferences: You can retrieve shared application preferences using the getSharedPreferences() method of the application Context. The SharedPreferences class can be used to save simple application data, such as configuration settings.

Accessing Other Application Functionality Using Context: The application Context provides access to a number of other top-level application features.

Here are a few more things you can do with the application Context:

- Launch Activity instances.

- Inspect and enforce application permissions.

- Retrieve assets packaged with the application.

- Request a system service (for example, location service).

- Manage private application files, directories, and databases.

Transition

In the course of the lifetime of an Android application, the user might transition between a numbers of different Activity instances. At times, there might be multiple Activity instances on the activity stack. Developers need to pay attention to the lifecycle of each Activity during these transitions.

Some Activity instances such as the application splash/startup screen are shown and then permanently discarded when the Main menu screen Activity takes over. The user cannot return to the splash screen Activity without re-launching the application. Other Activity transitions are temporary, such as a child Activity displaying a dialog box, and then returning to the original Activity (which was paused on the activity stack and now resumes). In this case, the parent Activity launches the child Activity and expects a result.

Transitioning between Activities with Intents: As previously mentioned, Android applications can have multiple entry points. There is nomain() function, such as you find in iPhone development. Instead, a specific Activity can be designated as the main Activity to launch by default within the AndroidManifest.xml file; Other Activities might be designated to launch under specific circumstances. For example, a music application might designate a generic Activity to launch by default from the Application menu, but also define specific alternative entry point Activities for accessing specific music playlists by playlist ID or artists by name.

Launching a New Activity by Class Name: You can start activities in several ways. The simplest method is to use the Application Context object to call the startActivity() method, which takes a single parameter, an Intent.

Intent (android.content.Intent) is an asynchronous message mechanism used by the Android operating system to match task requests with the appropriate Activity or Service (launching it, if necessary) and to dispatch broadcast Intents events to the system at large. For now, though, we focus on Intents and how they are used with Activities. The following line of code calls the startActivity() method with an explicit Intent. This Intent requests the launch of the target Activity named MyDrawActivity by its class.This class is implemented elsewhere within the package.
   startActivity(new Intent(getApplicationContext(), MyDrawActivity.class));

This line of code might be sufficient for some applications, which simply transition from one Activity to the next. However, you can use the Intent mechanism in a much more robust manner. For example, you can use the Intent structure to pass data between Activities.

Creating Intents with Action and Data: You've seen the simplest case to use Intent to launch a class by name. Intents need not specify the component or class they want to launch explicitly. Instead, you can create an Intent Filter and register it within the Android Manifest file.The Android operating system attempts to resolve the Intent requirements and launch the appropriate Activity based on the filter criteria. The guts of the Intent object are composed of two main parts: the action to be performed and the data to be acted upon. You can also specify action/data pairs using IntentAction types and Uri objects. An Uri object represents a string that gives the location and name of an object. Therefore, an Intent is basically saying "do this" (the action) to "that" (the Uri describing what resource to do the action to). The most common action types are defined in the Intent class, including ACTION_MAIN (describes the main entry point of an Activity) and ACTION_EDIT (used in conjunction with a Uri to the data edited).You also find Action types that generate integration points with Activities in other applications, such as the Browser or Phone Dialer.

Launching an Activity Belonging to another Application: Initially, your application might be starting only Activities defined within its own package. However, with the appropriate permissions, applications might also launch external Activities within other applications. For example, a Customer Relationship Management (CRM) application might launch the Contacts application to browse the Contact database, choose a specific contact, and return that Contact's unique identifier to the CRM application for use. Here is an example of how to create a simple Intent with a predefined Action(ACTION_DIAL) to launch the Phone Dialer with a specific phone number to dial in the form of a simple Uri object:

```
Uri number = Uri.parse(tel:5555551212);
Intent dial = new Intent(Intent.ACTION_DIAL, number);
startActivity(dial);
```

CHAPTER - 8
Working with Services

You can create your own services and use them to perform background tasks asynchronously. To improve application responsiveness and performance, consider implementing a service to handle the task outside the main application lifecycle. Any Services exposed by an Android application must be registered in the Android Manifest file.

Uses Services

- A weather, email, or social network app might implement a service to routinely check for updates.
- A photo or media app that keeps its data in sync online might implement a service to package and upload new content in the background when the device is idle.
- A video-editing app might offload heavy processing to a queue on its service in order to avoid affecting overall system performance for non-essential tasks.
- A news application might implement a service to "pre-load" content by downloading news stories in advance of when the user launches the application, to improve performance.

Creating a Service

To create service you must defined a class that extends the Service base class. Inside your service class, you have to implement four methods discussed below:

Method	Description
onStartCommand()	The system calls this method when another component, such as an activity, requests that the service be started, by calling startService(). Once this method executes, the service is started and can run in the background indefinitely. It is your responsibility to stop the service when its work is done, by calling stopSelf() or stopService(). If you only want to provide binding, you don't need to implement this method.
onBind()	The system calls this method when another component wants to bind with the service by calling bindService(). In your implementation of this method, you must provide an interface that clients use to communicate with the service, by returning an IBinder. If you don't want to allow binding, then you should return null.
onCreate()	The system calls this method when the service is first created, to perform one-time setup procedures before it calls either onStartCommand() or onBind(). If the service is already running, this method is not called.
onDestroy()	The system calls this method when the service is no longer used and is being destroyed. This method should be implemented to clean up any resources such as threads, registered listeners, receivers, etc. This is the last call the service receives.

Table-14

Start and Stop a Service

You can use Intents and Activities to launch services using the startService() and bindService() methods. A service can essentially take two forms. The difference between two is as follows:

startService()	bindService()
A service is "started" when an application component starts it by calling startService()	A service is "bound" when an application component binds to it by calling bindService()
Once started, a service can run in the background indefinitely, even if the component that started it is destroyed	A bound service runs only as long as another application component is bound to it. Multiple components can bind to the service.
Usually, a started service performs a single operation and does not return a result to the caller. For example, it might download or upload a file over the network. When the operation is done, the service should stop itself	A bound service offers a client-server interface that allows components to interact with the service, send requests, get results, and even do so across processes with inter process communication (IPC)

Table-15

Service Life Cycle

Like an activity, a service has lifecycle callback methods that you can implement to monitor changes in the service's state and perform work at the appropriate times as discussed above. Below figure illustrates the typical callback methods for a service for that are created by startService() and from those created by bindService.

Creating your own service

1. Create a New Android Studio Project with project name ServiceDemo and Main Activity name as ServiceActivity.
2. Add new service by right click on package and select New -> Service -> Service and click.

Figure-8a

3. In dialog box, Enter class name as TimerService as shown in figure and press finish Button.

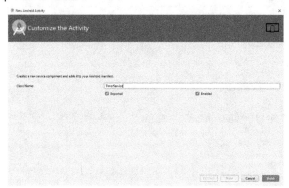

Figure-8b

4. Write following code inside TimerService class package in.ajitvoice.servicesdemo;

```
import android.util.Log; import android.widget.Toast;
import java.util.Timer; import java.util.TimerTask;
public class TimerService extends Service
{
    int counter = 0;
    Timer timer = new Timer();
```

31

```java
public TimerService() { }
@Override
public IBinder onBind(Intent intent) { return null;}
@Override
public int onStartCommand(Intent intent, int flags, int startId)
{
Toast.makeText (this, "Service Started!", Toast.LENGTH_LONG).show();
timer.scheduleAtFixedRate(new TimerTask() {
public void run()
{
    Log.d("MyService", String.valueOf(++counter));
}
}, 0, 1000);
return START_STICKY;
}
@Override
public void onDestroy()
{
super.onDestroy();
if (timer != null)
{
    timer.cancel();
}
Toast.makeText(this, "Service Destroyed!", Toast.LENGTH_LONG).show();
}
}
```

5. In android_service.xml file add the following statements in bold

```xml
<RelativeLayoutxmlns:android="http://schemas.android.com/apk/res/android"
xmlns:tools="http://schemas.android.com/tools"
android:layout_width="match_parent"
android:layout_height="match_parent"
android:paddingLeft="@dimen/activity_horizontal_margin"
android:paddingRight="@dimen/activity_horizontal_margin"
android:paddingTop="@dimen/activity_vertical_margin"
android:paddingBottom="@dimen/activity_vertical_margin"
tools:context=".ServiceActivity">
```

```xml
<TextViewandroid:text="Service Demonstration"
android:layout_width="match_parent" android:layout_height="wrap_content"
android:id="@+id/textView" />

<Button android:layout_width="match_parent"
android:layout_height="wrap_content" android:text="Start Timer Service"
android:id="@+id/btnStartTimer" android:layout_alignParentLeft="true"
android:layout_alignParentStart="true" android:layout_below="@+id/textView" />

<Button android:layout_width="match_parent"
android:layout_height="wrap_content" android:text="Stop Timer Service"
android:id="@+id/btnStopTimer" android:layout_below="@+id/btnStartTimer"
android:layout_alignParentLeft="true" android:layout_alignParentStart="true" />
</RelativeLayout>
```

6. Add the following statements in bold to the ServiceActivity.java file: package
in.ajitvoice.servicesdemo;
import android.content.Intent; import android.view.View; import
android.widget.Button;

```java
public class ServiceActivity extends ActionBarActivity
{
Button startTimer,stopTimer;
   @Override
protected void onCreate(Bundle savedInstanceState)
{
super.onCreate(savedInstanceState); setContentView(R.layout.activity_service);
startTimer = (Button)findViewById(R.id.btnStartTimer);
stopTimer = (Button)findViewById(R.id.btnStopTimer);
startTimer.setOnClickListener(new View.OnClickListener()
{ @Override
public void onClick(View v)
{
startService(new Intent(getBaseContext(), TimerService.class));
}
});
stopTimer.setOnClickListener(new View.OnClickListener()
{ @Override
   public void onClick(View v)
   {
```

```
        stopService(new Intent(getBaseContext(), TimerService.class));
    } });
}
```

7. Press Shift+F10 or 'Run App' button in taskbar. It will launch following dialog box. Press OK.

8. It will open activity in emulator as shown below. Clicking the **START TIMER SERVICE** button will start the service as shown below. To stop the service, click the **STOP TIMER SERVICE**.

9. Once service is started, you can see counter value incremented by in LogCat window.

Explanation

- Inside project layout file we created two buttons to start and stop service with ID btnStartTimer and btnStopTimer.
- Inside ServiceActivity we define two button objects that represents button in layout file.
- The findViewByID() method is used to take reference of button.
- Button clicked event is handled by onClick() method of OnClickListener associated to button using setOnClickListener().
- Inside TimerService class we define counter variable which initialized to zero at the start of service and increment by one every one second using Timer class scheduledAtFixedRate() Method.
- The value of counter is logs inside LogCat window using Log.d() Method with tag "MyService".
- Toast is temporary message displayed on screen such as "Service Started" and is displayed using makeText method of Toast class.

CHAPTER - 9

Working with Intent

Intent provides a facility for performing late runtime binding between the codes in different applications. Its most significant use is in the launching of activities, where it can be thought of as the glue between activities. It is basically a passive data structure holding an abstract description of an action to be performed.

Intent Structure

Intent has primary attributes which are mandatory and secondary attributes which are optional.

Primary Attributes

Primary Attributes: The primary pieces of information in intent are:

- Action: The general action to be performed, such as ACTION_VIEW, ACTION_EDIT, ACTION_MAIN, etc.
- Data: The data to operate on, such as a person record in the contacts database, expressed as an Uri.
- Some examples of action/data pairs are:
- ACTION_VIEW content://contacts/people/9 :Display information about the person whose identifier is "9".
- ACTION_DIAL content://contacts/people/9 :Display the phone dialer with the person filled in.
- ACTION_VIEW tel:123 : Display the phone dialer with the given number filled in. Note how the VIEW action does what is considered the most reasonable thing for a particular URI.
- ACTION_DIAL tel:123 : Display the phone dialer with the given number filled in.
- ACTION_EDIT content://contacts/people/9 : Edit information about the person whose identifier is "9".
- ACTION_VIEW content://contacts/people/ : Display a list of people, which the user can browse through. This example is a typical top-level entry into the Contacts application, showing you the list of people. Selecting a particular person to view would result in a new intent {ACTION_VIEWcontent://contacts/people/N } being used to start an activity to display that person.

Secondary Attributes

In addition to these primary attributes, there are a number of secondary attributes that you can also include with intent:

- **Category:** Gives additional information about the action to execute. For example, CATEGORY_LAUNCHER means it should appear in the Launcher as a top-level application, while CATEGORY_ALTERNATIVE means it should be included in a list of alternative actions the user can perform on a piece of data.

- **Type:** Specifies an explicit type (a MIME type) of the intent data. Normally the type is inferred from the data itself. By setting this attribute, you disable that evaluation and force an explicit type.

- **Component:** Specifies an explicit name of a component class to use for the intent. Normally this is determined by looking at the other information in the intent (the action, data/type, and categories) and matching that with a component that can handle it. If this attribute is set then none of the evaluation is performed, and this component is used exactly as is. By specifying this attribute, all of the other Intent attributes become optional.

- **Extras:** This is a Bundle of any additional information. This can be used to provide extended information to the component. For example, if we have a action to send an e-mail message, we could also include extra pieces of data here to supply a subject, body, etc.

Other Operations on Intent

- **ACTION_MAIN with category CATEGORY_HOME:** Launch the home screen.

- **ACTION_GET_CONTENT with MIME type vnd.android.cursor.item/phone:** Display the list of people's phone numbers, allowing the user to browse through them and pick one and return it to the parent activity.

- **ACTION_GET_CONTENT with MIME type */* and category CATEGORY_OPENABLE**: Display all pickers for data that can be opened and allowing the user to pick one of them and then some data inside of it and returning the resulting URI to the caller. This can be used, for example, in an e-mail application to allow the user to pick some data to include as an attachment.

There are a variety of standard Intent action and category constants defined in the Intent class, but applications can also define their own, for example, the standard ACTION_VIEW is called "android.intent.action.VIEW".

Types of Intent

There are two primary forms of intents you will use.

- **Explicit Intents** have specified a component which provides the exact class to be run. Often these will not include any other information, simply being a way for an application to launch various internal activities it has as the user interacts with the application.

- **Implicit Intents** have not specified a component; instead, they must include enough information for the system to determine which of the available components is best to run for that intent.

Intent Resolution

When using implicit intents, given such an arbitrary intent we need to know what to do with it. This is handled by the process of Intent resolution, which maps an Intent to an Activity, BroadcastReceiver, or Service that can handle it. The intent resolution mechanism basically revolves around matching Intent against all of the <intent-filter> descriptions in the installed application packages. There are three pieces of information in the Intent that are used for resolution: the action, type, and category. Using this information, a query is done on the PackageManager for a component that can handle the intent. The appropriate component is determined based on the intent information supplied in the AndroidManifest.xml file as follows:

- The action, if given, must be listed by the component as one it handles.
- The type is retrieved from the Intent's data, if not already supplied in the Intent. Like the action, if a type is included in the intent (either explicitly or implicitly in its data), then this must be listed by the component as one it handles.
- For data that is not a content: URI and where no explicit type is included in the Intent, instead the scheme of the intent data (such as http: or mailto:) is

considered. Again like the action, if we are matching a scheme it must be listed by the component as one it can handle.
- The categories, if supplied, must all be listed by the activity as categories it handles. That is, if you include the categories CATEGORY_LAUNCHER and CATEGORY_ALTERNATIVE, then you will only resolve to components with an intent that lists both of those categories. Activities will very often need to support the CATEGORY_DEFAULT so that they can be found by startActivity.

Types of Intent

For example, consider the Note Pad sample application that allows a user to browse through a list of notes data and view details about individual items.

```
<manifest xmlns:android="http://schemas.android.com/apk/res/android"
    package="in.ajitvoice.notepad">
<application android:icon="@drawable/app_notes"android:label="@string/app_name">
    <provider class=".NotePadProvider"android:authorities="in.ajitvoice.provider.NotePad" />
    <activity class=".NotesList" android:label="@string/title_notes_list">
    <intent-filter>
     <action android:name="android.intent.action.MAIN" />
        <category android:name="android.intent.category.LAUNCHER" />
    </intent-filter>
    <intent-filter>
        <action android:name="android.intent.action.VIEW" />
        <action android:name="android.intent.action.EDIT" />
        <action android:name="android.intent.action.PICK" />
        <category android:name="android.intent.category.DEFAULT" />
        <data android:mimeType="vnd.android.cursor.dir/vnd.google.note" />
    </intent-filter>
    <intent-filter>
        <action android:name="android.intent.action.GET_CONTENT" />
        <category android:name="android.intent.category.DEFAULT" />
        <data android:mimeType="vnd.android.cursor.item/vnd.google.note" />
    </intent-filter>
</activity>
<activity class=".NoteEditor" android:label="@string/title_note">
    <intent-filter android:label="@string/resolve_edit">
        <action android:name="android.intent.action.VIEW" />
```

```
                        <action android:name="android.intent.action.EDIT" />
                        <category android:name="android.intent.category.DEFAULT" />
                        <data android:mimeType="vnd.android.cursor.item/vnd.google.note" />
                </intent-filter>
                <intent-filter>
                        <action android:name="android.intent.action.INSERT" />
                        <category android:name="android.intent.category.DEFAULT" />
                        <data android:mimeType="vnd.android.cursor.dir/vnd.google.note" /
            </intent-filter>
        </activity>
        <activity class=".TitleEditor" android:label="@string/title_edit_title"
        android:theme="@android:style/Theme.Dialog">
                <intent-filter android:label="@string/resolve_title">
                        <action android:name="com.android.notepad.action.EDIT_TITLE" />
                        <category android:name="android.intent.category.DEFAULT" />
                        <category android:name="android.intent.category.ALTERNATIVE" />
        <category android:name="android.intent.category.SELECTED_ALTERNATIVE" />
                        <data android:mimeType="vnd.android.cursor.item/vnd.google.note" />
        </intent-filter>
        </activity>
        </application>
        </manifest>
```

Explanation of Example

In above example, the first activity, in.ajitvoice.provider.notepad,NotesList, serves as our main entry into the app. It can do three things as described by its three intent templates:

```
    <intent-filter>
    <action android:name="android.intent.action.MAIN" />
    <category android:name="android.intent.category.LAUNCHER" />
    </intent-filter>
```

This provides a top-level entry into the NotePad application: the standard MAIN action is a main entry point (not requiring any other information in the Intent), and the LAUNCHER category says that this entry point should be listed in the application launcher.

```
    <intent-filter>
    <action android:name="android.intent.action.VIEW" />
    <action android:name="android.intent.action.EDIT" />
```

39

```
<action android:name="android.intent.action.PICK" />
<category android:name="android.intent.category.DEFAULT" />
<data android:mimeType="vnd.android.cursor.dir/vnd.google.note" />
</intent-filter>
```

This declares the things that the activity can do on a directory of notes. The type being supported is given with the <type> tag, where vnd.android.cursor.dir/vnd.google.note is a URI from which a Cursor of zero or more items (vnd.android.cursor.dir) can be retrieved which holds our note pad data (vnd.google.note). The activity allows the user to view or edit the directory of data (via the VIEW and EDIT actions), or to pick a particular note and return it to the caller (via the PICK action). Note also the DEFAULT category supplied here: this is required for the startActivity method to resolve your activity when its component name is not explicitly specified.

```
<intent-filter>
<action android:name="android.intent.action.GET_CONTENT" />
<category android:name="android.intent.category.DEFAULT" />
<data android:mimeType="vnd.android.cursor.item/vnd.google.note" />
</intent-filter>
```

This filter describes the ability to return to the caller a note selected by the user without needing to know where it came from. The data type vnd.android.cursor.item/vnd.google.note is a URI from which a Cursor of exactly one (vnd.android.cursor.item) item can be retrieved which contains our note pad data (vnd.google.note). The GET_CONTENT action is similar to the PICK action, where the activity will return to its caller a piece of data selected by the user. Here, however, the caller specifies the type of data they desire instead of the type of data the user will be picking from.

Given these capabilities, the following intents will resolve to the NotesList activity:

- **{ action=android.app.action.MAIN }** matches all of the activities that can be used as top-level entry points into an application.
- **{ action=android.app.action.MAIN, category=android.app.category.LAUNCHER }** is the actual intent used by the Launcher to populate its top-level list.
- **{ action=android.intent.action.VIEW data=content://com.google.provider.NotePad/notes }** displays a list of all the

notes under "content://com.google.provider.NotePad/notes", which the user can browse through and see the details on

- { action=android.app.action.PICK data=content://com.google.provider.NotePad/notes } provides a list of the notes under "content://com.google.provider.NotePad/notes", from which the user can pick a note whose data URL is returned back to the caller.
- { action=android.app.action.GET_CONTENTtype=vnd.android.cursor.item/vnd. google.note } is similar to the pick action, but allows the caller to specify the kind of data they want back so that the system can find the appropriate activity to pick something of that data type.
- The second activity, in.ajitvoice.notepad.NoteEditor, shows the user a single note entry and allows them to edit it. It can do two things as described by its two intent templates:

<intent-filter android:label="@string/resolve_edit">

<action android:name="android.intent.action.VIEW" />

<action android:name="android.intent.action.EDIT" />

<category android:name="android.intent.category.DEFAULT" />

<data android:mimeType="vnd.android.cursor.item/*vnd.google.note*" />

</intent-filter>

The first, primary, purpose of this activity is to let the user interact with a single note, as described by the MIME type vnd.android.cursor.item/vnd.google.note. The activity can either VIEW a note or allow the user to EDIT it. Again we support the DEFAULT category to allow the activity to be launched without explicitly specifying its component.

<intent-filter>

<action android:name="android.intent.action.INSERT" />

<category android:name="android.intent.category.DEFAULT" />

<data android:mimeType="vnd.android.cursor.dir/vnd.google.note" />

</intent-filter>

The secondary use of this activity is to insert a new note entry into an existing directory of notes. This is used when the user creates a new note: the INSERT action is executed on the directory of notes, causing this activity to run and have the user create the new note data which it then adds to the content provider.

Given these capabilities, the following intents will resolve to the NoteEditor activity:

- **{ action=android.app.action.EDIT data=content://in.ajitvoice.provider.NotePad/notes/** *{ID}***}** allows the user to edit the content of note *{ID}*.
- **{action=android.intent.action.VIEW data=content://in.ajitvoice.provider.NotePad/notes/{ID}}** shows the user the content of note {ID}.
- **{ action=android.app.action.INSERT data=content://in.ajitvoice.provider.NotePad/notes }** creates a new, empty note in the notes list at "content://com.google.provider.NotePad/notes" and allows the user to edit it. If they keep their changes, the URI of the newly created note is returned to the caller.
- The last activity, com.android.notepad.TitleEditor, allows the user to edit the title of a note. This could be implemented as a class that the application directly invokes (by explicitly setting its component in the Intent), but here we show a way you can publish alternative operations on existing data:

<intent-filter android:label="@string/resolve_title">
<action android:name="com.android.notepad.action.EDIT_TITLE" />
<category android:name="android.intent.category.DEFAULT" />
<category android:name="android.intent.category.ALTERNATIVE" />
<category android:name="android.intent.category.SELECTED_ALTERNATIVE" />
<data android:mimeType="vnd.android.cursor.item/vnd.google.note" />
</intent-filter>

- In the single intent template here, we have created our own private action called com.android.notepad.action.EDIT_TITLE which means to edit the title of a note. It must be invoked on a specific note like the previous view and edit actions, but here displays and edits the title contained in the note data.
- In addition to supporting the default category as usual, our title editor also supports two other standard categories: ALTERNATIVE and SELECTED_ALTERNATIVE. Implementing these categories allows others to find the special action it provides without directly knowing about it, through the PackageManager.queryIntentActivityOptions(ComponentName, Intent[ ], Intent, int) method, or more often to build dynamic menu items with Menu.addIntentOptions (int, int, int, ComponentName, Intent[ ], Intent, int, MenuItem[ ]). Note that in the intent template here was also supply an explicit

42

name for the template (via android:label="@string/resolve_title") to better control what the user sees when presented with this activity as an alternative action to the data they are viewing.

- Given these capabilities, the following intent will resolve to the TitleEditor activity:

- {action=com.android.notepad.action.EDIT_TITLE data=content://com.google.provider.NotePad/notes/*{ID}*} displays and allows the user to edit the title associated with note *{ID}*.

Standard Activity Actions

Frequently used, are ACTION_MAIN and ACTION_EDIT.

ACTION_MAIN	ACTION_DIAL	ACTION_RUN
ACTION_VIEW	ACTION_CALL	ACTION_SYNC
ACTION_ATTACH_DATA	ACTION_SEND	ACTION_PICK_ACTIVITY
ACTION_EDIT ACTION_PICK	ACTION_SENDTO	ACTION_SEARCH
ACTION_CHOOSER	ACTION_ANSWER	ACTION_WEB_SEARCH
ACTION_GET_CONTENT	ACTION_INSERT	ACTION_FACTORY_TEST
	ACTION_DELETE	

Standard Broadcast Actions

(usually through registerReceiver or a <receiver> tag in a manifest).

ACTION_TIME_TICK	ACTION_PACKAGE_DATA_CLEARED
ACTION_TIME_CHANGED	ACTION_PACKAGES_SUSPENDED
ACTION_TIMEZONE_CHANGED	ACTION_PACKAGES_UNSUSPENDED
ACTION_BOOT_COMPLETED	ACTION_UID_REMOVED
ACTION_PACKAGE_ADDED	ACTION_BATTERY_CHANGED
ACTION_PACKAGE_CHANGED	ACTION_POWER_CONNECTED
ACTION_PACKAGE_REMOVED	ACTION_POWER_DISCONNECTED
ACTION_PACKAGE_RESTARTED	ACTION_SHUTDOWN

CHAPTER - 10
Permissions in Android

A permission is to protect the privacy of an Android user. Android apps must request permission to access sensitive user data (such as contacts and SMS), as well as certain system features (such as camera and internet). Depending on the feature, the system might grant the permission automatically or might prompt the user to approve the request.

A central design point of the Android security architecture is that no app, by default, has permission to perform any operations that would adversely impact other apps, the operating system, or the user. This includes reading or writing the user's private data (such as contacts or emails), reading or writing another app's files, performing network access, keeping the device awake, and so on.

This CHAPTER provides an overview of how Android permissions work, including: how permissions are presented to the user, the difference between install-time and runtime permission requests, how permissions are enforced, and the types of permissions and their groups.

Permission Approval

```
<manifest xmlns:android="http://schemas.android.com/apk/res/android"
package="in.ajitvoice.myapp">
<uses-permission android:name="android.permission.SEND_SMS"/>
<application ...>

    ...

</application>
</manifest>
```

If your app lists normal permissions in its manifest (that is, permissions that don't pose much risk to the user's privacy or the device's operation), the system automatically grants those permissions to your app.

If your app lists dangerous permissions in its manifest (that is, permissions that could potentially affect the user's privacy or the device's normal operation), such as the SEND_SMS permission above, the user must explicitly agree to grant those permissions.

Request prompts for dangerous permissions

Only dangerous permissions require user agreement. The way Android asks the user to grant dangerous permissions depends on the version of Android running on the user's device, and the system version targeted by your app.

Runtime requests (Android 6.0 and higher)

If the device is running Android 6.0 (API level 23) or higher, and the app's targetSdkVersion is 23 or higher, the user isn't notified of any app permissions at install time. Your app must ask the user to grant the dangerous permissions at runtime. When your app requests permission, the user sees a system dialog as shown in figure 10a telling the user which permission group your app is trying to access. The dialog includes a Deny and Allow button. If the user denies the permission request, the next time your app requests the permission, the dialog contains a checkbox that, when checked, indicates the user doesn't want to be prompted for the permission again.

Figure-10a

If the user checks the Never ask again box and taps Deny, the system no longer prompts the user if you later attempt to requests the same permission.

Even if the user grants your app the permission it requested you cannot always rely on having it. Users also have the option to enable and disable permissions one-by-one in system settings. You should always check for and request permissions at runtime to guard against runtime errors (SecurityException).

Install-time requests (Android 5.1.1 and below)

If the device is running Android 5.1.1 (API level 22) or lower, or the app's targetSdkVersion is 22 or lower while running on any version of Android, the system automatically asks the user to grant all dangerous permissions for your app at install- time as shown in figure 10b.

Figure-10b

If the user clicks Accept, all permissions the app requests are granted. If the user denies the permissions request, the system cancels the installation of the app.
If an app update includes the need for additional permissions the user is prompted to accept those new permissions before updating the app.

Permissions for optional hardware features

Access to some hardware features such as Bluetooth or the camera requires app permission. However, not all Android devices actually have these hardware features. So if your app requests the CAMERA permission, it's important that you also include the <uses-feature> tag in your manifest to declare whether or not this feature is actually required. For example:

```
<uses-feature android:name="android.hardware.camera"
android:required="false" />
```

If you declare android:required="false" for the feature, then Google Play allows your app to be installed on devices that don't have the feature. You then must check if the current device has the feature at runtime by calling PackageManager.hasSystemFeature(), and gracefully disable that feature if it's not available.

If you don't provide the <uses-feature> tag, then when Google Play sees that your app requests the corresponding permission, it assumes your app requires this feature. So it filters your app from devices without the feature, as if you declared android:required="true" in the <uses-feature> tag.

Custom App Permission

Permissions aren't only for requesting system functionality. Services provided by apps can enforce custom permissions to restrict who can use them.

Activity permission enforcement

Permissions applied using the android:permission attribute to the <activity> tag in the manifest restrict who can start that Activity. The permission is checked during Context.startActivity() and Activity.startActivityForResult(). If the caller doesn't have the required permission then SecurityException is thrown from the call.

Service permission enforcement

Permissions applied using the android:permission attribute to the <service> tag in the manifest restrict who can start or bind to the associated Service. The permission is checked during Context.startService(), Context.stopService() and Context.bindService(). If the caller doesn't have the required permission then SecurityException is thrown from the call.

Broadcast permission enforcement

Permissions applied using the android:permission attribute to the <receiver> tag restrict who can send broadcasts to the associated BroadcastReceiver. The permission is checked after Context.sendBroadcast() returns, as the system tries to deliver the submitted broadcast to the given receiver. As a result, a permission failure doesn't result in an exception being thrown back to the caller; it just doesn't deliver the Intent.

In the same way, a permission can be supplied to Context.registerReceiver() to control who can broadcast to a programmatically registered receiver. Going the other way, a permission can be supplied when calling Context.sendBroadcast() to restrict which broadcast receivers are allowed to receive the broadcast.

Note that both a receiver and a broadcaster can require permission. When this happens, both permission checks must pass for the intent to be delivered to the associated target.

Content Provider permission enforcement

Permissions applied using the android:permission attribute to the <provider> tag restrict who can access the data in a ContentProvider. Unlike the other components, there are two separate permission attributes you can set: android:readPermission restricts who can read from the provider, and android:writePermission restricts who can write to it. Note that if a provider is protected with both a read and write permission, holding only the write permission doesn't mean you can read from a provider.

The permissions are checked when you first retrieve a provider and as you perform operations on the provider.

Using ContentResolver.query() requires holding the read permission;
using ContentResolver.insert(), ContentResolver.update(), ContentResolver.delete() requires the write permission. In all of these cases, not holding the required permission results in a SecurityException being thrown from the call.

URI Permissions

The standard permission system described so far is often not sufficient when used with content providers. A content provider may want to protect itself with read and write permissions, while its direct clients also need to hand specific URIs to other apps for them to operate on.

A typical example is attachments in a email app. Access to the emails should be protected by permissions, since this is sensitive user data. However, if a URI to an image attachment is given to an image viewer, that image viewer no longer has permission to open the attachment since it has no reason to hold a permission to access all email.

The solution to this problem is per-URI permissions: when starting an activity or returning a result to an activity, the caller can set
Intent.FLAG_GRANT_READ_URI_PERMISSION and/or
Intent.FLAG_GRANT_WRITE_URI_PERMISSION.
This grants the receiving activity permission access the specific data URI in the intent, regardless of whether it has any permission to access data in the content provider corresponding to the intent.

This mechanism allows a common capability style model where user interaction (such as opening an attachment or selecting a contact from a list) drives ad-hoc granting of fine grained permission. This can be a key facility for reducing the permissions needed by apps to only those directly related to their behavior.

To build the most secure implementation that makes other apps accountable for their actions within your app, you should use fine-grained permissions in this manner and declare your app's support for it with the android:grantUriPermissions attribute or <grant-uri-permissions> tag.

Other permission enforcement

Arbitrarily fine-grained permissions can be enforced at any call into a service. This is accomplished with the Context.checkCallingPermission() method. Call with a desired permission string and it returns an integer indicating whether that permission has been granted to the current calling process. Note that this can only be used when you are executing a call coming in from another process, usually through an IDL interface published from a service or in some other way given to another process.

There are a number of other useful ways to check permissions. If you have the process ID (PID) of another process, you can use the Context.checkPermission() method to check a permission against that PID. If you have the package name of another app, you can use the PackageManager.checkPermission() method to find out whether that particular package has been granted a specific permission.

Permission Protection levels

Permissions are divided into several protection levels. The protection level affects whether runtime permission requests are required.

There are three protection levels that affect third-party apps: normal, signature, and dangerous permissions.

Normal permissions

Normal permissions cover areas where your app needs to access data or resources outside the app's sandbox, but where there's very little risk to the user's privacy or the operation of other apps. For example, permission to set the time zone is a normal permission.

If an app declares in its manifest that it needs a normal permission, the system automatically grants the app that permission at install time. The system doesn't prompt the user to grant normal permissions, and users cannot revoke these permissions.

As of Android 9 (API level 28), the following permissions are classified as PROTECTION_NORMAL:

ACCESS_LOCATION_EXTRA_COMMANDS
ACCESS_NETWORK_STATE
ACCESS_NOTIFICATION_POLICY
ACCESS_WIFI_STATE
BLUETOOTH BLUETOOTH_ADMIN BROADCAST_STICKY CHANGE_NETWORK_STATE
CHANGE_WIFI_MULTICAST_STATE CHANGE_WIFI_STATE DISABLE_KEYGUARD
EXPAND_STATUS_BAR FOREGROUND_SERVICE GET_PACKAGE_SIZE INSTALL_SHORTCUT
INTERNET KILL_BACKGROUND_PROCESSES
MANAGE_OWN_CALLS MODIFY_AUDIO_SETTINGS NFC READ_SYNC_SETTINGS
READ_SYNC_STATS
RECEIVE_BOOT_COMPLETED REORDER_TASKS REQUEST_DELETE_PACKAGES
SET_ALARM
SET_WALLPAPER SET_WALLPAPER_HINTS TRANSMIT_IR USE_FINGERPRINT VIBRATE
WAKE_LOCK WRITE_SYNC_SETTINGS

Signature permissions

The system grants these app permissions at install time, but only when the app that attempts to use permission is signed by the same certificate as the app that defines the permission.

As of Android 8.1 (API level 27), the following permissions that third-party apps can use are classified as PROTECTION_SIGNATURE:

BIND_ACCESSIBILITY_SERVICE BIND_AUTOFILL_SERVICE BIND_CARRIER_SERVICES
BIND_CHOOSER_TARGET_SERVICE BIND_CONDITION_PROVIDER_SERVICE
BIND_DEVICE_ADMIN BIND_DREAM_SERVICE BIND_INCALL_SERVICE BIND_INPUT_METHOD
BIND_MIDI_DEVICE_SERVICE BIND_NFC_SERVICE BIND_NOTIFICATION_LISTENER_SERVICE
BIND_PRINT_SERVICE BIND_SCREENING_SERVICE BIND_TELECOM_CONNECTION_SERVICE
BIND_TEXT_SERVICE
BIND_TV_INPUT BIND_VISUAL_VOICEMAIL_SERVICE BIND_VOICE_INTERACTION
BIND_VPN_SERVICE BIND_VR_LISTENER_SERVICE BIND_WALLPAPER CLEAR_APP_CACHE
MANAGE_DOCUMENTS READ_VOICEMAIL REQUEST_INSTALL_PACKAGES
SYSTEM_ALERT_WINDOW WRITE_SETTINGS
WRITE_VOICEM

Dangerous permissions

Dangerous permissions cover areas where the app wants data or resources that involve the user's private information, or could potentially affect the user's stored data or the operation of other apps. For example, the ability to read the user's contacts is a dangerous permission. If an app declares that it needs a dangerous permission, the user has to explicitly grant the permission to the app. Until the user approves the permission, your app cannot provide functionality that depends on that permission.

Special permissions

There are a couple of permissions that don't behave like normal and dangerous permissions. SYSTEM_ALERT_WINDOW and WRITE_SETTINGS are particularly sensitive, so most apps should not use them. If an app needs one of these permissions, it must declare the permission in the manifest, and send an intent requesting the user's authorization. The system responds to the intent by showing a detailed management screen to the user.

How to View app's permissions

You can view all the permissions currently defined in the system using the Settings app and the shell command adb shell pm list permissions. To use the Settings app, go to Settings > Apps. Pick an app and scroll down to see the permissions that the app uses. For developers, the adb '-s' option displays the permissions in a form similar to how the user sees them:

```
$ adb shell pm list permissions -s All Permissions:

Network communication: view Wi-Fi state, create Bluetooth connections,
fullinternet access, view network state

Your location: access extra location provider commands, fine (GPS)
location,mock location sources for testing, coarse (network-based) location

Services that cost you money: send SMS messages, directly call phone
numbers

...
```

You can also use the adb -g option to grant all permissions automatically when installing an app on an emulator or test device:

```
$ adb shell install -g MyApp.apk
```

Android Manifest File Application Property Elements

1. <uses-permission>: The <uses-permission> tag is used to specify the in-app permissions that your app would require for proper functioning. By default, many of the permissions are kept as false for security purposes.

2. <permission>: The <permission> tag is used to provide access to control some of the app's components.

3. <permission-groups>:You can group several such permissions using <permission-group>.

0

4. <permission-tree>: The <permission-tree> tag specifies the particular component that owns the other components.

5. <instrumentation>: The <instrumentation> tag is used to specify the type of interaction between the application and the system.

6. <uses-sdk>: The <uses-sdk> specifies the version of SDK on which the app is compatible.

7. <uses-configuration>: The <uses-configuration> tag is used to specify the permissions that are required to maintain the security and integrity of your application.

8. <uses-feature>: The <uses-feature> is used to specify the specific hardware or software requirements for your application.

9. <supports-screen, compatible-screen>: It allows you to specify supported screen sizes for your application.

Permissions in Manifest File

Permissions are quite an essential aspect of the manifest file. Suppose you are developing a picture capturing and editing application. Now your application needs access to your camera. Now, if you need camera access, you need to seek permission from the user. After the user grants then only your application can access the camera to capture pictures.

Initially, the app has some permissions set to true, while most are set to false to avoid security issues.

Some of the permissions which are by default true are as follows:

INTERNET
ACCESS_NETWORK_STATE
READ_PHONE_STATE

Now, let's see how you can specify the permissions for your application. You need to use the <uses-permission> to specify the permission you wish to have in your application.

Code:

```
<manifest >
<uses-permission .../>
...
<manifest >
```

Now let's see the list of permissions that are by default false and require you to make them true if we need them explicitly.

ACCESS_WIFI_STATE
AUTHENTICATE_ACCOUNT
BLUETOOTH
BATTERY_STATS
BIND_APPWIDGET
BROADCAST_WAP_PUSH
BROADCAST_STICKY
BIND_INPUT_METHOD
CALL_PHONE
CHANGE_CONFIGURATION
CAMERA
CLEAR_APP_DATA
CHANGE_WIFI_STATE
CLEAR_APP_USER_DATA
DEVICE_POWER
DELETE_CACHE_FILES
DISABLE_KEYGUARD
DELETE_PACKAGES
EXPAND_STATUS_BAR
EXPAND_STATUS_BAR
FACTORY_TEST
GET_PACKAGE_SIZE
FLASHLIGHT
GLOBAL_SEARCH
HARDWARE_TEST
INTERNAL_SYSTEM_PROCESSES
USE_CREDENTIALS
MANAGE_ACCOUNTS
MANAGE_APP_TOKENS

2

MODIFY_AUDIO_SETTINGS
MODIFY_PHONE_STATE
NFC
SEND_SMS
PROCESS_OUTGOING_CALLS
SET_ALARM
SET_ALWAYS_FINISH
READ_CALENDAR
KILL_BACKGROUND_PROCESSES
SET_WALLPAPER
VIBRATE
WAKE_LOCK
WRITE_APN_SETTINGS
WRITE_CALENDAR
WARITE_SETTINGS

Intent-Filters

Intent-Filters are used to trigger the app components like Activity, Service, Receiver etc. When the app issues an intent towards an app component, the system locates the app component and performs the desired action provided by the intent filter. The action to be performed, data, or the intended message is carried through an object known as an intent object.
In the manifest file, you use the <intent-filter> tag to make intent to app components.

For example, you can see below the intent filter for activities.

Code:

```
<activity
      android:name=".MainActivity"
      android:exported="true">
      <intent-filter>
        <action android:name="android.intent.action.MAIN" />

        <category android:name="android.intent.category.LAUNCHER" />
      </intent-filter>
  </activity>
```

CHAPTER - 11
Application Resources

You should always externalize app resources such as images and strings from your code, so that you can maintain them independently. You should also provide alternative resources for specific device configurations, by grouping them in specially named resource directories. At runtime, Android uses the appropriate resource based on the current configuration. For example, you might want to provide a different UI layout depending on the screen size or different strings depending on the language setting.

Once you externalize your app resources, you can access them using resource IDs that are generated in your project's R class. This document shows you how to group your resources in your Android project and provide alternative resources for specific device configurations, and then access them from your app code or other XML files. The well written application accesses its resources programmatically instead of hard coding them into the source code. This is done for a variety of reasons. Storing application resources in a single place is a more organized approach to development and makes the code more readable and maintainable. Externalizing resources such as strings makes it easier to localize applications for different languages and geographic regions.

What are resources?

All Android applications are composed of two things: functionality (code instructions) and data (resources). The functionality is the code that determines how your application behaves. This includes any algorithms that make the application run. Resources include textstrings, images and icons, audio files, videos, and other data used by the application.Android resource files are stored separately from the java class files in the Android project.Most common resource types are stored in XML. You can also store raw data files

Resource Directory Hierarchy

Each resource type corresponds to a specific resource subdirectory name. For example, all graphics are stored under the /res/drawable directory structure. Resources can be further organized in a variety of ways using even more specially named directory qualifiers.

For example, the /res/drawable-hdpi directory stores graphics for high density screens, the /res/drawable-ldpi directory stores graphics for low density screens, and the /res/drawable-mdpi directory stores graphics for medium-density screens. If you had a graphic resource that was shared by all screens, you would simply store that resource in the/res/drawable directory.

Resource Value Types

Android applications rely on many different types of resources such as text strings, graphics, and color schemes for user interface design.

These resources are stored in the /res directory of your Android project in a strict (but reasonably flexible) set of directories and files. All resources filenames must be lowercase and simple (letters, numbers, and underscores only).
The resource types supported by the Android SDK and how they are stored within the project are shown in table below

Resource Type	Directory	Filename	XML Tag
Strings	/res/values/	strings.xml	<string>
StringPluralization	/res/values/	strings.xml	<plurals>, <item>
Arrays ofStrings	/res/values/	strings.xml	<string-array>,<item>
Booleans	/res/values/	bools.xml	<bool>
Colors	/res/values/	Colors.xml	<color>

Color StateLists	/res/color/	Examples include buttonstates.xml indicators.xml	<selector>, <item>
Dimensions	/res/values/	Dimens.xml	<dimen>
Integers	/res/values/	integers.xml	<integer>
Resource Type	Directory	Filename	XML Tag
Arrays of Integers	/res/values/	integers.xml	<integer-array>,<item>
Mixed-Type Arrays	/res/values/	Arrays.xml	<array>, <item>
SimpleDrawables	/res/values/	drawables.xml	<drawable>
Graphics	/res/drawable/	Examples include icon.png logo.jpg	Supported graphics files or drawable definition XML files such as shapes.
TweenedAnimations	/res/anim/	Examples include fadesequence.xml spinsequence.xml	<set>, <alpha>, <scale>, <translate>, <rotate>
Frame-by-Frame Animations	/res/drawable/	Examples include sequence1.xml sequence2.xml	<animation-list>, <item>
Menus	/res/menu/	Examples include mainmenu.xml helpmenu.xml	<menu>
XML Files	/res/xml/	Examples include data.xml data2.xml	Defined by the developer
Raw Files	/res/raw/	Examples include jingle.mp3 somevideo.mp4 helptext.txt	Defined by the developer
Layouts	/res/layout/	Examples include main.xml help.xml	Varies. Must be a layout control.
Styles andThemes	/res/values/	styles.xml themes.xml	<style>

Table-17

Storing Different Resource Value Types

Storing Simple Resource Types Such as Strings

Simple resource value types, such as strings, colors, dimensions, and other primitives, are stored under the /res/values project directory in XML files. Each resource file under the /res/values directory should begin with the following XML header:

<?xml version="1.0" encoding="utf-8"?>

Next comes the root node <resources> followed by the specific resource element types such as <string> or <color>. Each resource is defined using a different element name. Although the XML file names are arbitrary, the best practice is to store your resources in separate files to reflect their types, such as strings.xml, colors.xml, and so on. However,there's nothing stopping the developers from creating multiple resource files for a given type, such as two separate xml files called bright_colors.xml andmuted_colors.xml, if they so choose.

Storing Graphics, Animations, Menus, and Files

In addition to simple resource types stored in the /res/values directory, you can also store numerous other types of resources, such as animation sequences, graphics, arbitrary XML files, and raw files. These types of resources are not stored in the /res/values directory,but instead stored in specially named directories according to their type. For example,you can include animation sequence definitions in the /res/anim directory. Make sure you name resource files appropriately because the resource name is derived from the filename of the specific resource. For example, a file called flag.png in the/res/drawable directory is given the name R.drawable.flag.

Accessing Resource Programmatically

When android application is compiled, a R class gets generated, which contains resource IDs for all the resources available in your res/ directory. You can use R class to access that resource using sub-directory and resource name or directly resource ID.

During your application development you will need to access defined resources either in your code, or in your layout XML files. Following section explains how to access your resources in both the scenarios.

Example-1: To access res/drawable/myimage.png and set an ImageView you will use following code –

```
ImageView imageView = (ImageView) findViewById(R.id.myimageview);
imageView.setImageResource(R.drawable.myimage);
```

Here first line of the code make use of R.id.myimageview to get ImageView defined with id myimageview in a Layout file. Second line of code makes use of R.drawable.myimage to get an image with name myimage available in drawable sub-directory under /res.

Example-2: Consider next example where res/values/strings.xml has following definition:

```
<?xml version="1.0" encoding="utf-8"?>
<resources>
<string name="hello">Hello, World!</string>
</resources>
```

Now you can set the text on a TextView object with ID msg using a resource ID as follows:

```
TextView msgTextView = (TextView) findViewById(R.id.msg);
msgTextView.setText(R.string.hello);
```

Example-3: Consider a layout res/layout/activity_main.xml with the following definition:

1

```xml
<?xml version="1.0" encoding="utf-8"?>
<LinearLayoutxmlns:android="http://schemas.android.com/apk/res/android"
android:layout_width="fill_parent"
android:layout_height="fill_parent" android:orientation="vertical" >
<TextViewandroid:id="@+id/text" android:layout_width="wrap_content"
android:layout_height="wrap_content" android:text="Hello, I am a TextView" />
<Button android:id="@+id/button" android:layout_width="wrap_content"
android:layout_height="wrap_content" android:text="Hello, I am a Button" />
</LinearLayout>
```

This application code will load this layout for an Activity, in the onCreate() method as follows:

```java
public void onCreate(Bundle savedInstanceState)
{
super.onCreate(savedInstanceState); setContentView(R.layout.activity_main);
}
```

Accessing Resources in XML Layout

Consider the following resource XML res/values/strings.xml file that includes a color resource and a string resource:

```xml
<?xml version="1.0" encoding="utf-8"?>

<resources>

<color name="opaque_red">#f00</color>

<string name="hello">Hello!</string>

</resources>
```

Now you can use these resources in the following layout file to set the text color and text string as follows:

```xml
<?xml version="1.0" encoding="utf-8"?>

<EditTextxmlns:android="http://schemas.android.com/apk/res/android"
android:layout_width="fill_parent"
android:layout_height="fill_parent" android:textColor="@color/opaque_red"
android:text="@string/hello" />
```

Referencing System Resources

You can access system resources in addition to your own resources. The android package contains all kinds of resources, which you can browse by looking in the android.R subclasses.Here you find system resources for

- Animation sequences for fading in and out
- Arrays of email/phone types (home, work, and such)
- Standard system colors
- Dimensions for application thumbnails and icons
- Many commonly used drawable and layout types
- Error strings and standard button text
- System styles and themes

You can reference system resources the same way you use your own; set the package name to android. For example, to set the background to the system color for darker gray, you set the appropriate background color attribute to @android:color/darker_gray.

You can access system resources much like you access your application's resources. Instead of using your application resources, use the Android package's resources under the android.R class.

CHAPTER - 12
User Interface Screen Elements

Android applications inevitably need some form of user interface. In this CHAPTER, we will discuss the user interface elements available within the Android Software Development Kit (SDK). Some of these elements display information to the user, whereas others gather information from the user.

You learn how to use a variety of different components and controls to build a screen and how your application can listen for various actions performed by the user. Finally, you learn how to style controls and apply themes to entire screens.

Introduction to Views, Controls and Layout

Let's talk about the View class.

Introduction to Android Views

A View is a simple building block of a user interface. It is a small rectangular box that can be TextView, EditText, or even a button. It occupies the area on the screen in a rectangular area and is responsible for drawing and event handling. View is a superclass of all the graphical user interface components. This class represents the basic building block for user interface components. A View occupies a rectangular area on the screen and is responsible for drawing and event handling. View is the base class for widgets, which are used to create interactive UI components (buttons, text fields, etc.). The ViewGroup subclass is the base class for layouts, which are invisible containers that hold other Views (or other ViewGroups) and define their layout properties.

All of the views in a window are arranged in a single tree. You can add views either from code or by specifying a tree of views in one or more XML layout files. There are many specialized subclasses of views that act as controls or are capable of displaying text, images, or other content.

0

Now you might be thinking what is the use of a View. So, the use of a view is to draw content on the screen of the user's Android device. A view can be easily implemented in an Application using the java code. Its creation is more easy in the XML layout file of the project. Like, the project for hello world that we had made initially. Once you have created a tree of views, there are typically a few types of common operations you may wish to perform:

Set properties: for example setting the text of a TextView. The available properties and the methods that set them will vary among the different subclasses of views. Note that properties that are known at build time can be set in the XML layout files.

Set focus: The framework will handle moving focus in response to user input. To force focus to a specific view, call requestFocus().

Set up listeners: Views allow clients to set listeners that will be notified when something interesting happens to the view. For example, all views will let you set a listener to be notified when the view gains or loses focus. You can register such a listener using setOnFocusChangeListener (android.view.View.OnFocusChangeListener).
Other view subclasses offer more specialized listeners. For example, a Button exposes a listener to notify clients when the button is clicked.

Set visibility: You can hide or show views using setVisibility(int).

Types of Android Views

Another thing that might now come to your mind must be, "what are the available types of view in Android that we can use?" For that, we'll see all these types one by one as follows:
- TextView
- EditText
- Button
- Image Button
- Date Picker
- RadioButton
- CheckBox buttons
- Image View

And there are some more components.

1

Introduction to Android Controls

The Android SDK contains a Java package named android.widget. When we refer to controls, we are typically referring to a class within this package. The Android SDK includes classes to draw most common objects, including ImageView, FrameLayout, EditText, and Button classes. All controls are typically derived from the View class. We cover many of these basic controls in detail.

Introduction to Android Layout

One special type of control found within the android.widget package is called a layout. A layout control is still a View object, but it doesn't actually draw anything specific on the screen. Instead, it is a parent container for organizing other controls (children). Layout controls determine how and where on the screen child controls are drawn. Each type of layout control draws its children using particular rules. For instance, the LinearLayoutcontrol draws its child controls in a single horizontal row or a single vertical column. Similarly, a TableLayout control displays each child control in tabular format (in cells within specific rows and columns).

By necessity, we use some of the layout View objects within this CHAPTER to illustrate how to use the controls previously mentioned. However, we don't go into the details of the various layout types available as part of the Android SDK until the next CHAPTER. We will lean in more details about layout in next CHAPTER.

TextView

TextView is a user interface element that displays text to the user. Following table shows important XML Attributes of TextView control.

Attribute	Description
id	id is an attribute used to uniquely identify a text view
gravity	The gravity attribute is an optional attribute which is used to control the alignment of the text like left, right, center, top, bottom, center_vertical, center_horizontal etc.
text	text attribute is used to set the text in a text view.
textColor	textColor attribute is used to set the text color of a text view. Color value is in the form of "#argb", "#rgb", "#rrggbb", or "#aarrggbb".
textSize	textSize attribute is used to set the size of text of a text view. We can set the text size in sp(scale independent pixel) or dp(density pixel).
textStyle	textStyle attribute is used to set the text style of a text view. The possible text styles are bold, italic and normal.
background	background attribute is used to set the background of a text view. We can set a color or a drawable in the background of a text view
padding	padding attribute is used to set the padding from left, right, top or bottom.

Table-18

3

The following code sample shows a typical use, with an XML layout and code to modify the contents of the text view:

```
<LinearLayout xmlns:android="http://schemas.android.com/apk/res/android"
android:layout_width="match_parent" android:layout_height="match_parent">
<TextView
        android:id="@+id/text_view_id" android:layout_width="wrap_content"
        android:layout_height="wrap_content" android:text="This is TextView"
        android:layout_centerInParent="true" android:textSize="35sp"
        android:padding="15dp" android:textColor="#aaa"
        android:background="#fff"/>
</LinearLayout>
```

This code sample demonstrates how to modify the contents of the text view defined in the previous XML layout:

```
public class MainActivity extends Activity {
    protected void onCreate(Bundle savedInstanceState)
    { super.onCreate(savedInstanceState); setContentView(R.layout.activity_main);
        final TextView helloTextView = (TextView) findViewById(R.id.text_view_id);
        helloTextView.setText(R.string.user_greeting);

    }

}
```

To display this TextView on the screen, all your Activity needs to do is call the setContentView() method with the layout resource identifier in which you defined in the preceding XML shown.

You can change the text displayed programmatically by calling the setText() method on the TextView object. Retrieving the text is done with the getText() method. To customize the appearance of TextView we can use Styles and Themes.

EditText

EditText is a user interface element for entering and modifying text.Following table shows important XML Attributes of EditText control.

Attribute	Description
id	This is an attribute used to uniquely identify an edit text
gravity	The gravity attribute is an optional attribute which is used to control the alignment of the text like left, right, center, top, bottom, center_vertical, center_horizontal etc.
text	This attribute is used to set the text in a text view.
hint	It is an attribute used to set the hint i.e. what you want user to enter in this edit text. Whenever user start to type in edit text the hint will automatically disappear.
lines	Define show many lines tall the input box is. If this is not set, the entry field grows as the user enters text.
textColorHint	It is an attribute used to set the color of displayed hint.
textColor	This attribute is used to set the text color of a edit text. Color value is in the form of "#argb", "#rgb", "#rrggbb", or "#aarrggbb".
textSize	This attribute is used to set the size of text of a edit text. We can set the text size in sp(scale independent pixel) or dp(density pixel).
textStyle	This attribute is used to set the text style of a edit text. The possible text styles are bold, italic and normal.
background	This attribute is used to set the background of a edit text. We can set a color or a drawable in the background of a edit text
padding	Padding attribute is used to set the padding from left, right, top or bottom.

Table-19

Following layout code shows a basic EditText element.
```
<EditText android:id="@+id/txtName"
android:layout_height="wrap_content" android:hint="Full Name" android:lines="4"
android:layout_width="fill_parent" />
```

5

The EditText object is essentially an editable TextView. You can read text from it in by using the getText() method. You can also set initial text to draw in the text entry area using the setText() method.You can also highlight a portion of the text from code by call to setSelection() method and a call to selectAll() method highlights the entire text entry field.

By default, the user can perform a long press to bring up a context menu. This provides to the user some basic copy, cut, and paste operations as well as the ability to change the input method and add a word to the user's dictionary of frequently used words. You can set the editable attribute to false, so the user cannot edit the text in the field but can still copy text out of it using a long press.

AutoCompleteTextView

In Android, AutoCompleteTextView is a view i.e. similar to EditText, except that it displays a list of completion suggestions automatically while the user is typing. A list of suggestions is displayed in drop down menu from which user can choose an item which actually replace the content of EditBox with that.
It is a subclass of EditText class so we can inherit all the properties of EditText in a AutoCompleteTextView.
Following layout code shows a basic AutoComplete TextView element.

```
<AutoCompleteTextView android:id="@+id/ac" android:layout_width="fill_parent"
android:layout_height="wrap_content" android:text=" Auto Suggestions
EditText"/>
```

To display the Array content in an AutoCompleteTextView we need to implement Adapter. In AutoCompleteTextView we mainly display text values so we use Array Adapter when we need list of single type of items which is backed by an Array. For example, list of phone contacts, countries or names.
```
ArrayAdapter(Context context, int resource, int textViewResourceId, T[ ] objects)
AutoCompleteTextView ac = (AutoCompleteTextView) findViewById(R.id.ac);
```

Following code retrieve the value from a AutoCompleteTextView in Java class.

```
String v = ac.getText().toString();
```

Spinner

In Android, Spinner provides a quick way to select one value from a set of values. It is similar to dropdown list in other programming language. In a default state, a spinner shows its currently selected value. It provides an easy way to select a value from a known set.Following table shows important XML Attributes of spinner control.

Attribute	Description
dropDownHorizontalOffset	Amount of pixels by which the drop down should be offset horizontally.
dropDownSelector	List selector to use for spinnerMode="dropdown" display.
	May be a reference to another resource, in the form "@[+][package:]type/name" or a theme attribute in the form "?[package:]type/name".
	May be a color value, in the form of "#rgb", "#argb", "#rrggbb", or "#aarrggbb".
dropDownVerticalOffset	Amount of pixels by which the drop down should be offset vertically.
dropDownWidth	Width of the dropdown in spinnerMode="dropdown".
gravity	Gravity setting for positioning the currently selected item.
popupBackground	Background drawable to use for the dropdown in spinnerMode="dropdown".
prompt	The prompt to display when the spinner's dialog is shown.
spinnerMode	Display mode for spinner options. Must be one of the following constant values.

Constant	Value	Description
dialog	0	Spinner options will be presented to the user as a dialog window.
dropdown	1	Spinner options will be presented to the user as an inline dropdown anchored to the spinner widget itself.

Table-20

0

As with the auto-complete method, the possible choices for a spinner can come from an Adapter. You can also set the available choices in the layout definition by using the entries attribute with an array resource. Following is an XML layout for showing spinner

<Spinner android:id="@+id/Spinner01" android:layout_width="wrap_content"
android:layout_height="wrap_content" android:entries="@array/colors"
android:prompt="@string/spin_prompt" />

This places a Spinner control on the screen.When the user selects it, a pop-up shows the prompt text followed by a list of the possible choices. This list allows only a single item to be selected at a time, and when one is selected, the pop-up goes away. First, the entries attribute is set to the values that shows by assigning it to an array resource, referred to here as @array/colors.

Populate the Spinner with User Choices

The choices you provide for the spinner can come from any source, but must be provided through a SpinnerAdapter, such as an ArrayAdapter if the choices are available in an array or a CursorAdapter if the choices are available from a database query.

For instance, if the available choices for your spinner are pre-determined, you can provide them with a string array defined in a string resource file:

```
<?xml version="1.0" encoding="utf-8"?>
<resources>
<string-array name="planets_array">
    <item>Mercury</item>
    <item>Venus</item>
    <item>Earth</item>
    <item>Mars</item>
    <item>Jupiter</item>
    <item>Saturn</item>
    <item>Uranus</item>
    <item>Neptune</item>
  </string-array>
</resources>
```

With an array such as this one, you can use the following code in your <u>Activity</u> or <u>Fragment</u> to supply the spinner with the array using an instance of <u>ArrayAdapter</u>:

Spinner spinner = (Spinner) findViewById(R.id.spinner);

// Create an ArrayAdapter using the string array and a default spinner layout
ArrayAdapter<CharSequence> adapter = ArrayAdapter.createFromResource(this, R.array.planets_array, android.R.layout.simple_spinner_item);

// Specify the layout to use when the list of choices appears
adapter.setDropDownViewResource(android.R.layout.simple_spinner_dropdown_item);

// Apply the adapter to the spinner spinner.setAdapter(adapter);

The createFromResource() method allows you to create an ArrayAdapter from the string array. The third argument for this method is a layout resource that defines how the selected choice appears in the spinner control. The simple_spinner_item layout is provided by the platform and is the default layout you should use unless you'd like to define your own layout for the spinner's appearance.

You should then call setDropDownViewResource(int) to specify the layout the adapter should use to display the list of spinner choices.

Call setAdapter() to apply the adapter to your Spinner.

Responding to User Selections

When the user selects an item from the drop-down, the Spinner object receives an onItemSelected event.

To define the selection event handler for a spinner, implement the AdapterView.OnItemSelectedListener interface and the corresponding onItemSelected() callback method. For example, here's an implementation of the interface in an Activity:

2

```java
public class SpinnerActivity extends Activity implements
OnItemSelectedListener
{
    ...

    public void onItemSelected(AdapterView<?> parent, View view, int pos, long id)
    {
        // An item was selected. You can retrieve the selected item using
        // parent.getItemAtPosition(pos)
    }

    public void onNothingSelected(AdapterView<?> parent)
    {
        // Another interface callback
    }
}
```

The AdapterView.OnItemSelectedListener requires the onItemSelected() and onNothingSelected() callback methods.
Then you need to specify the interface implementation by calling setOnItemSelectedListener():

```java
Spinner spinner = (Spinner) findViewById(R.id.spinner);
spinner.setOnItemSelectedListener(this);
```

If you implement the AdapterView.OnItemSelectedListener interface with your Activity or Fragment (such as in the example above), you can pass this as the interface instance.

Button

A user interface element the user can tap or click to perform an action. To display a button in an activity, add a button to the activity's layout XML file:

```
<Button
    android:layout_width="wrap_content" android:layout_height="wrap_content"
    android:text="@string/button_text"
    android:drawableLeft="@drawable/button_icon"
    ... />
```

To specify an action when the button is pressed, set a click listener on the button object in the corresponding activity code:

Figure-12a

```
public class MyActivity extends Activity
{
protected void onCreate(Bundle savedInstanceState)
{
super.onCreate(savedInstanceState);
setContentView(R.layout.content_layout_id);
final Button button = findViewById(R.id.button_id);
button.setOnClickListener(new View.OnClickListener()
{
        public void onClick(View v)
        {
        // Code here executes on main thread after user presses button
        }
    });
}}
```

4

The above snippet creates an instance of View.OnClickListener and wires the listener to the button using setOnClickListener (View.OnClickListener). As a result, the system executes the code you write in onClick(View) after the user presses the button.

Every button is styled using the system's default button background, which is often different from one version of the platform to another. If you are not satisfied with the default button style, you can customize it.

Checkbox

A checkbox is a specific type of two-states button that can be either checked or unchecked.

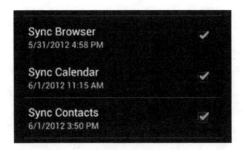

Figure-12b

To create each checkbox option, create a CheckBox in your layout. Because a set of checkbox options allows the user to select multiple items, each checkbox is managed separately and you must register a click listener for each one.

Responding to Click Events

When the user selects a checkbox, the CheckBox object receives an on-click event. To define the click event handler for a checkbox, add the android:onClick attribute to the <CheckBox> element in your XML layout. The value for this attribute must be the name of the method you want to call in response to a click event. The Activity hosting the layout must then implement the corresponding method.

For example, here are a couple CheckBox objects in a list:

```
<?xml version="1.0" encoding="utf-8"?>

    <LinearLayoutxmlns:android="http://schemas.android.com/apk/res/android"
        android:orientation="vertical"
        android:layout_width="fill_parent" android:layout_height="fill_parent">
```

6

```xml
<CheckBoxandroid:id="@+id/checkbox_meat"
    android:layout_width="wrap_content" android:layout_height="wrap_content"
    android:text="@string/meat" android:onClick="onCheckboxClicked"/>
<CheckBoxandroid:id="@+id/checkbox_cheese"
    android:layout_width="wrap_content" android:layout_height="wrap_content"
    android:text="@string/cheese" android:onClick="onCheckboxClicked"/>
</LinearLayout>
```

Within the Activity that hosts this layout, the following method handles the click event for both checkboxes:

```java
public void onCheckboxClicked(View view)
{
    // Is the view now checked?
    boolean checked = ((CheckBox) view).isChecked();
    // Check which checkbox was clicked switch(view.getId())
    {
        case R.id.checkbox_meat: if (checked)
            // Put some meat on the sandwich else
            // Remove the meat break;
        case R.id.checkbox_cheese: if (checked)
            // Cheese me else
            // I'm lactose intolerant break;
        // TODO: Veggie sandwich
    }
}
```

Radio Button

Radio buttons allow the user to select one option from a set. You should use radio buttons for optional sets that are mutually exclusive if you think that the user needs to see all available options side-by-side. If it's not necessary to show all options side-by-side, use a spinner instead.

To create each radio button option, create a RadioButton in your layout. However, because radio buttons are mutually exclusive, you must group them together inside a RadioGroup. By grouping them together, the system ensures that only one radio button can be selected at a time.

Responding to Click Events

When the user selects one of the radio buttons, the corresponding RadioButton object receives an on-click event.

To define the click event handler for a button, add the android:onClick attribute to the <RadioButton> element in your XML layout. The value for this attribute must be the name of the method you want to call in response to a click event. The Activity hosting the layout must then implement the corresponding method.

For example, here are a couple RadioButton objects:

```
<?xml version="1.0" encoding="utf-8"?>
<RadioGroupxmlns:android="http://schemas.android.com/apk/res/android"
android:layout_width="match_parent" android:layout_height="wrap_content"
android:orientation="vertical">
<RadioButtonandroid:id="@+id/radio_pirates"
android:layout_width="wrap_content" android:layout_height="wrap_content"
android:text="@string/pirates" android:onClick="onRadioButtonClicked"/>
<RadioButtonandroid:id="@+id/radio_ninjas"
android:layout_width="wrap_content" android:layout_height="wrap_content"
android:text="@string/ninjas" android:onClick="onRadioButtonClicked"/>
</RadioGroup>
```

Within the Activity that hosts this layout, the following method handles the click event for both radio buttons:

```java
public void onRadioButtonClicked(View view)
{
    // Is the button now checked?
boolean checked = ((RadioButton) view).isChecked();.
    // Check which radio button was clicked switch(view.getId())
    {
        case R.id.radio_pirates: if (checked)
            // Pirates are the best break;
        case R.id.radio_ninjas: if (checked)
            // Ninjas rule break;
    }

}
```

Date

Android provides controls for the user to pick a time or pick a date as ready-to-use dialogs. Each picker provides controls for selecting each part of the time (hour, minute, AM/PM) or date (month, day, year). Using these pickers helps ensure that your users can pick a time or date that is valid, formatted correctly, and adjusted to the user's locale.

Figure-12d

It is recommended that you use DialogFragment to host each time or date picker. The DialogFragment manages the dialog lifecycle for you and allows you to display the pickers in different layout configurations, such as in a basic dialog on handsets or as an embedded part of the layout on large screens.

Creating a Time Picker

To display a TimePickerDialog using DialogFragment, you need to define a fragment class that extends DialogFragment and return a TimePickerDialog from the fragment's onCreateDialog() method.

Extending DialogFragment for a time picker

To define a DialogFragment for a TimePickerDialog, you must:

- Define the onCreateDialog() method to return an instance of TimePickerDialog.

- Implement the TimePickerDialog.OnTimeSetListener interface to receive a callback when the user sets the time.

Here's an example:

```
public static class TimePickerFragment extends DialogFragment implements
            TimePickerDialog.OnTimeSetListener
{
    @Override
    public Dialog onCreateDialog(Bundle savedInstanceState)
    {
        // Use the current time as the default values for the picker
        final Calendar c = Calendar.getInstance();
        int hour = c.get(Calendar.HOUR_OF_DAY); int minute =
        c.get(Calendar.MINUTE);
        // Create a new instance of TimePickerDialog and return it return new
        TimePickerDialog(getActivity(), this, hour, minute,
        DateFormat.is24HourFormat(getActivity())));
    }
    public void onTimeSet(TimePicker view, int hourOfDay, int minute)
    {
        // Do something with the time chosen by the user
    }
}
```

Showing the time picker

Once you've defined a DialogFragment like the one shown above, you can display the time picker by creating an instance of the DialogFragment and calling show(). For example, here's a button that, when clicked, calls a method to show the dialog:

```
<Button android:layout_width="wrap_content"
android:layout_height="wrap_content"
android:text="@string/pick_time" android:onClick="showTimePickerDialog" />
```

When the user clicks this button, the system calls the following method:

```
public void showTimePickerDialog(View v)
{
DialogFragment newFragment = new TimePickerFragment();
newFragment.show(getSupportFragmentManager(), "timePicker");
}
```

This method calls show() on a new instance of the DialogFragment defined above. The show() method requires an instance of FragmentManager and a unique tag name for the fragment.

Creating a Date Picker

Creating a DatePickerDialog is just like creating a TimePickerDialog. The only difference is the dialog you create for the fragment.
To display a DatePickerDialog using DialogFragment, you need to define a fragment class that extends DialogFragment and return a DatePickerDialog from the fragment's onCreateDialog() method.

Extending DialogFragment for a date picker

To define a DialogFragment for a DatePickerDialog, you must:

- Define the onCreateDialog() method to return an instance of DatePickerDialog.
- Implement the DatePickerDialog.OnDateSetListener interface to receive a callback when the user sets the date.

Here's an example:

```
public static class DatePickerFragment extends DialogFragment implements
DatePickerDialog.OnDateSetListener
{
      @Override
      public Dialog onCreateDialog(Bundle savedInstanceState)
      {
```

```
// Use the current date as the default date in the picker

final Calendar c = Calendar.getInstance();
int year = c.get(Calendar.YEAR);

int month = c.get(Calendar.MONTH);

int day = c.get(Calendar.DAY_OF_MONTH);

// Create a new instance of DatePickerDialog and return it

return new DatePickerDialog(getActivity(), this, year, month, day);
}
public void onDateSet(DatePicker view, int year, int month, int day)
{
// Do something with the date chosen by the user
}}
```

Showing the date picker

Once you've defined a DialogFragment like the one shown above, you can display the date picker by creating an instance of the DialogFragment and calling show(). For example, here's a button that, when clicked, calls a method to show the dialog:

```
<Button android:layout_width="wrap_content" android:layout_height="wrap_content"
android:text="@string/pick_date" android:onClick="showDatePickerDialog" />
```

When the user clicks this button, the system calls the following method:

```
public void showDatePickerDialog(View v)
{
DialogFragmentnewFragment = new DatePickerFragment();
newFragment.show(getSupportFragmentManager(), "datePicker");
}
```

This method calls show() on a new instance of the DialogFragment defined above. The show() method requires an instance of Fragment Manager and a unique tag name for the fragment.

Get current time and date on Android

SimpleDateFormat is a concrete class for formatting and parsing dates in a locale-sensitive manner. In this example, we have imported simple date format class from java as shown below -
import java.text.SimpleDateFormat;
import java.util.Date;

Step 1 – Create a new project in Android Studio, go to File ⇒ New Project and fill all required details to create a new project.

Step 2 – Add the following code to res/layout/activity_main.xml.

```
<?xml version="1.0" encoding="utf-8"?>
<RelativeLayout xmlns:android="http://schemas.android.com/apk/res/android"
  xmlns:app="http://schemas.android.com/apk/res-auto"
  xmlns:tools="http://schemas.android.com/tools"
  android:layout_width="match_parent"
  android:gravity="center"
  android:layout_height="match_parent">
  <TextView
    android:id="@+id/date"
    android:layout_width="wrap_content"
    android:layout_height="wrap_content"
    android:layout_centerHorizontal="true"
    android:textSize="30sp"
    android:layout_marginBottom="36dp" />
</RelativeLayout>
```

In the above code, we have given text view, it going to print the current date on the window manager.

Step 3 – Add the following code to src/MainActivity.java

```
package in.ajitvoice.myapplication;
import android.annotation.TargetApi;
import android.os.Build;
import android.os.Bundle;
```

```
import android.support.v7.app.AppCompatActivity;
import android.widget.TextView;
import java.text.SimpleDateFormat;
import java.util.Date;
public class MainActivity extends AppCompatActivity {
  @TargetApi(Build.VERSION_CODES.O)
  @Override
  protected void onCreate(Bundle savedInstanceState) {
    super.onCreate(savedInstanceState);
    setContentView(R.layout.activity_main);
    TextView textView=findViewById(R.id.date);
    SimpleDateFormat sdf = new SimpleDateFormat("yyyy.MM.dd G 'at' HH:mm:ss z");
    String currentDateandTime = sdf.format(new Date());
    textView.setText(currentDateandTime);
  }
}
```

In the above code we are calling SimpleDateFormat and from the simpledateformat, we are accessing the current date in the string. There are so many date format are available.

Step 4 – No need to change manifest.xml.

Let's try to run your application. I assume you have connected your actual Android Mobile device with your computer. To run the app from an android studio, open one of your project's activity files and click Run from the toolbar. Select your mobile device as an option and then check your mobile device which will display your default screen –

Figure-12e

15

ImageView

Adding an ImageView to an Activity

Whenever ImageView is added to an activity, it means there is a requirement for an image resource. Thus it is oblivious to provide an Image le to that ImageView class. It can be done by adding an image le that is present in the Android Studio itself or we can add our own image le. Android Studio owns a wide range of drawable resources which are very common in the android application layout. The following are the steps to add a drawable resource to the ImageView class.

Open the activity_main.xml File in which the Image is to be Added

Figure-12f

Switch from the Code View to the Design View of the activity_main.xml File

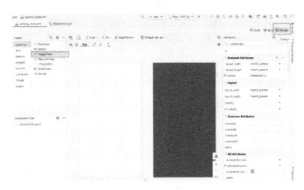

Figure-12g

16

For adding an image from Android Studio, Drag the ImageView widget to the activity area of the application, a pop-up dialogue box will open choose from the wide range of drawable resources and click "OK".

Figure-12h

For Adding an Image File other than Android Studio Drawable Resources:

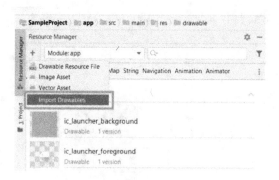

Figure-12i

Click on the **"Resource Manager"** tab on the leftmost panel and select the **"Import Drawables"** option.

Figure-12j

Select the path of the image le on your computer and click **"OK"**. After that set, the **"Qualifier type"** and **"value"** of the image le according to your need and click **"Next"** then **"Import"**.

Drag the ImageView class in the activity area, a pop-up dialogue box will appear which contains your imported image le. Choose your image le and click "OK", your image will be added to the activity.

Note: After adding an image set its constraints layout both vertically and horizontally otherwise it will show an error.

Step by Step Implementation

Step 1: Create a New Project

To create a new project in Android Studio please refer to How to Create/Start a New Project in Android Studio.

Step 2: Working with the activity_main.xml File Working with the activity_main.xml File

Go to the activity_main.xml File and refer to the following code. Below is the code for the activity_main.xml File.

Navigate to the app > res > layout > activity_main.xml and add the below code to that le. Below is the code for the activity_main.xml le.

```xml
<?xml version="1.0" encoding="utf-8"?>
<androidx.constraintlayout.widget.ConstraintLayout
    xmlns:android="http://schemas.android.com/apk/res/android"
    xmlns:app="http://schemas.android.com/apk/res-auto"
    xmlns:tools="http://schemas.android.com/tools"
    android:layout_width="match_parent"
    android:layout_height="match_parent"
    tools:context=".MainActivity">

    <ImageView
        android:id="@+id/GfG_full_logo" android:layout_width="0dp"
        android:layout_height="wrap_content" app:layout_constraintBottom_toBottomOf="parent"
        app:layout_constraintEnd_toEndOf="parent" app:layout_constraintStart_toStartOf="parent"
        app:layout_constraintTop_toTopOf="parent" app:layout_constraintVertical_bias="0.078"
        app:srcCompat="@drawable/full_logo" />

    <ImageView
        android:id="@+id/GfG_logo" android:layout_width="wrap_content"
        android:layout_height="wrap_content" app:layout_constraintBottom_toBottomOf="parent"
        app:layout_constraintEnd_toEndOf="parent" app:layout_constraintStart_toStartOf="parent"
        app:layout_constraintTop_toBottomOf="@+id/GfG_full_logo"
        app:srcCompat="@drawable/logo" />
</androidx.constraintlayout.widget.ConstraintLayout>
```

Note: All the attributes of the ImageView which are starting with app:layout_constraint are the vertical and horizontal constraints to x the image position in the activity. This is very necessary to add the constraint to the ImageView otherwise, all the images will take the position (0, 0) of the activity layout.

Step 4: Working with the MainActivity File

Go to the MainActivity le and refer to the following code. Below is the code for the MainActivity le. Since in the activity, only 2 images have been added and nothing else is being done like touching a button, etc. So, the MainActivity le will simply look like the below code i.e. no change.

```java
import androidx.appcompat.app.AppCompatActivity;
import android.os.Bundle;
public class MainActivity extends AppCompatActivity {
    @Override
    protected void onCreate(Bundle savedInstanceState) {
```

```
    super.onCreate(savedInstanceState);
    setContentView(R.layout.activity_main);

}}
```

Alert Dialog Box

Alert Dialog shows the Alert message and gives the answer in the form of yes or no. Alert Dialog displays the message to warn you and then according to your response, the next step is processed. Android Alert Dialog is built with the use of three fields: Title, Message area, and Action Button.

Alert Dialog code has three methods:

- setTitle() method for displaying the Alert Dialog box Title
- setMessage() method for displaying the message
- setIcon() method is used to set the icon on the Alert dialog box.

Then we add the two Buttons, setPositiveButton and setNegativeButton to our Alert Dialog Box as shown below.

Example:

Figure-12I

Step By Step Implementation

Step 1: Create a New Project in Android Studio

Step 2: Working with the XML Files
Next, go to the activity_main.xml file, which represents the UI of the project. Below is the code for the activity_main.xml file. Comments are added inside the code to understand the code in more detail.

```
<?xml version="1.0" encoding="utf-8"?>
<RelativeLayout xmlns:android="http://schemas.android.com/apk/res/android"
    xmlns:tools="http://schemas.android.com/tools"
    android:layout_width="match_parent"
    android:layout_height="match_parent"
```

20

```
    tools:context=".MainActivity">


<TextView
    android:layout_width="wrap_content"
    android:layout_height="wrap_content"
    android:layout_marginTop="180dp"
    android:gravity="center_horizontal"
    android:text="Press The Back Button of Your Phone."
    android:textSize="30dp"
    android:textStyle="bold" />

</RelativeLayout>
```

Step 3: Working with the MainActivity File
Go to the MainActivity File and refer to the following code. Below is the code for the MainActivity File. Comments are added inside the code to understand the code in more detail.

```
import android.content.DialogInterface;
import android.os.Bundle;
import androidx.appcompat.app.AlertDialog;
import androidx.appcompat.app.AppCompatActivity;

public class MainActivity extends AppCompatActivity {

  @Override
  protected void onCreate(Bundle savedInstanceState) {
    super.onCreate(savedInstanceState);
    setContentView(R.layout.activity_main);

  }

    // Declare the onBackPressed method when the back button is pressed this method will
call
  @Override
  public void onBackPressed() {
    // Create the object of AlertDialog Builder class
    AlertDialog.Builder builder = new AlertDialog.Builder(MainActivity.this);
    // Set the message show for the Alert time

    builder.setMessage("Do you want to exit ?");
    // Set Alert Title
    builder.setTitle("Alert !");
    // Set Cancelable false for when the user clicks on the outside the Dialog Box then it will
remain show
    builder.setCancelable(false);
    // Set the positive button with yes name Lambda OnClickListener method is use of
DialogInterface interface.
    builder.setPositiveButton("Yes", (DialogInterface.OnClickListener) (dialog, which) -> {
      // When the user click yes button then app will close m
      finish();
    });
```

```
        // Set the Negative button with No name Lambda OnClickListener method is use of
DialogInterface interface.
        builder.setNegativeButton("No", (DialogInterface.OnClickListener) (dialog, which) -> {
            // If user click no then dialog box is canceled.
            dialog.cancel();

        });

        // Create the Alert dialog
        AlertDialog alertDialog = builder.create();
        // Show the Alert Dialog box
        alertDialog.show();

    }
}
```

Figure-12m

Adapter

An adapter basically connects the User Interfaces and the Data Source. According to Android officials, "An Adapter object acts as a bridge between an AdapterView and the data for that view. Android Adapters basically provides access to the data items."

So we know, an adapter implements the Adapter Interface and acts as a link between a data set and an adapter view. An AdapterView is an object of a class extending the abstract AdapterView class. Now when we talk about the data, it can be anything that is present in Structured Manner. It also retrieves data from data set & generates view objects based on that data. It shows the data in different views like GridView, ListView, Spinners, etc.

What is an Adapter?

An adapter acts like a bridge between a data source and the user interface. It reads data from various data sources, coverts it into View objects and provide it to the linked Adapter view to create UI components.

The data source or dataset can be an Array object, a List object etc.

You can create your own Adapter class by extending the BaseAdapter class, which is the parent class for all other adapter class. Android SDK also provides some ready-to-use adapter classes, such as ArrayAdapter, SimpleAdapter etc.

What is an Adapter View?

An Adapter View can be used to display large sets of data efficiently in form of List or Grid etc, provided to it by an Adapter.

When we say efficiently, what do we mean?

An Adapter View is capable of displaying millions of items on the User Interface, while keeping the memory and CPU usage very low and without any noticeable lag. Different Adapters follow different strategies for this, but the default Adapter provided in Android SDK follow the following tricks:

It only renders those View objects which are currently on-screen or are about to some on-screen. Hence no matter how big your data set is, the Adapter View will always load only 5 or 6 or maybe 7 items at once, depending upon the display size. Hence saving memory.

It also reuses the already created layout to populate data items as the user scrolls, hence saving the CPU usage.

Suppose you have a dataset, like a String array with the following contents.

String days[ ] = {"Monday", "Tuesday", "Wednesday", "Thursday", "Friday", "Saturday", "Sunday"};

Now, what does an Adapter do is that it takes the data from this array and creates a View from this data and then, it gives this View to an AdapterView. The AdapterView then displays the data in the way you want.

Adapter is only responsible for taking the data from a data source and converting it into View and then passing it to the AdapterView. Thus, it is used to manage the data. AdapterView is responsible for displaying the data.

Therefore, you can take the data from a database or an ArrayList or any other data source and then, you can display that data in any arrangement. You can display it vertically (ListView), or in rows and columns (GridView), or in drop-down menu (Spinners), etc.

An Adapter View is capable of displaying millions of items on the User Interface, while keeping the memory and CPU usage very low and without any noticeable lag. Different Adapters follow different strategies for this, but the default Adapter provided in Android SDK follow the following tricks:

Adapters in Android

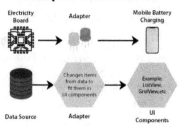

Figure-12n

Adapter View in Android

An Adapter View displays the set of data in the form of List or Grid provided by the Adapter. It has the capability to display a large number of items on the User Interface efficiently. An Android Adapter is responsible for taking the data from the source and put it in the AdapterView. And it is the responsibility of AdapterView to display the data. Adaptors help us make the user interface interactive and friendly to use.

An android adapte views can display the data on the Display screen in three forms that are:

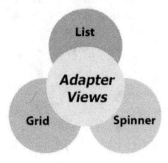

Figure-12o

Types of Android Adapters

Figure-12p

Android provides us with following different types of Adapters that are used to fill the data in UI components:

- BaseAdapter – BaseAdapter is the parent adapter for the rest of the Adapters.
- CursorAdapter – This adapter makes it easy and more controlled to access the binding of data values.
- ArrayAdapter – ArrayAdapter presents the items in a single list backed by an array.
- Custom ArrayAdapter – It displays the custom list of an Array.
- SimpleAdapter – SimpleAdapter is an easy adapter to map static data to the views through the XML file.
- Custom SimpleAdapter – It displays a customized list and enables us to access the child data of the list or grid view.

Implementation of Adapters in Android

Now we will implement it in our application using the following steps:

Step 1. First of all, we will create a new project and name it. I have named my application "My Adapter".

Step 2. Next we will create the layout for it in the activity_main.xml file:

```
<LinearLayout     xmlns:android="http://schemas.android.com/apk/res/android"
    xmlns:tools="http://schemas.android.com/tools"
    android:layout_width="match_parent"
    android:layout_height="match_parent"
    android:orientation="vertical"
```

```
tools:context=".MainActivity">

<TextView
    android:id="@+id/tV1"
    android:layout_width="wrap_content"
    android:layout_height="wrap_content"
    android:layout_centerHorizontal="true"
    android:layout_marginLeft="90dp"
    android:layout_marginTop="40dp"
    android:fontFamily="@font/amarante"
    android:text="ajitvoice"
    android:textColor="@color/colorPrimaryDark"
    android:textSize="50dp" />

<ListView
    android:id="@+id/Dog_List"
    android:layout_width="match_parent"
    android:layout_height="wrap_content"></ListView>

</LinearLayout>
```

Step 3. We will write the following code in the MainActivity.java file.

```
package in.ajitvoice.myadapter;
import android.os.Bundle;
import android.widget.ArrayAdapter;
import android.widget.ListView;
import androidx.appcompat.app.AppCompatActivity;
public class MainActivity extends AppCompatActivity {
 String[ ] Dogs = {"Husky", "Labrador", "Chow Chow", " Beagle ", " Rottweiler ", "
Doberman ", "Chihuahua", " Pit Bull ", "Pug", "Golden Retriever ", "German Shepherd",
"Great Dane", "Boxer"};
  @Override
  protected void onCreate(Bundle savedInstanceState) {
    super.onCreate(savedInstanceState);
    setContentView(R.layout.activity_main);
    ArrayAdapter my_adapter = new ArrayAdapter<String>(this,
        R.layout.my_list, Dogs);
    ListView List = findViewById(R.id.Dog_List);
    List.setAdapter(my_adapter);
  }
}
```

Step 4. Now we will create a file to customize the listview that would be shown. For that create a file my_list.xml and write the following code.

```xml
<?xml version="1.0" encoding="utf-8"?>
<TextView xmlns:android="http://schemas.android.com/apk/res/android"
  android:id="@+id/customize"
  android:layout_width="fill_parent"
  android:layout_height="fill_parent"
  android:fontFamily="@font/amiri"
  android:padding="10dp"
  android:textColor="#4A0505"
  android:textSize="20dp"
  android:textStyle="bold">
</TextView>
```

Step 5. After writing this, we will run the code:
This is the ListView.

Android Custom ListView with Image and Text

By creating a custom ListView you can design how a single row will look like in the view. ListView is the basic component to view the data in a list.

Steps and Source Code for Creating Custom ListView with image and text.

– First Create a new Project CustomListViewExample.
– Create an empty activity i.e MainActivity
– Add all images to res > drawable folder that are to be displayed in our ListView.
– Now add ListView to your Activity layout file

activity_main.xml file:

```
<?xml version="1.0" encoding="utf-8"?>
<RelativeLayout xmlns:android="http://schemas.android.com/apk/res/android"
xmlns:app="http://schemas.android.com/apk/res-auto"
xmlns:tools="http://schemas.android.com/tools"
android:layout_width="match_parent"
android:layout_height="match_parent"
tools:context="in.ajitvoice.customlistviewexample.MainActivity">

<ListView
android:id="@+id/androidList"
android:layout_width="match_parent"
android:layout_height="match_parent"/>

</RelativeLayout>
```

– Next step is to create a custom layout file to format how a single row will look in our ListView.
– Right click on the layout folder, New and then click on Layout resource file and name it to single_list_item.xml

single_list_item.xml file:

```
<?xml version="1.0" encoding="utf-8"?>
<RelativeLayout xmlns:android="http://schemas.android.com/apk/res/android"
android:layout_width="match_parent"
```

```
android:layout_height="match_parent"
android:padding="8dp">

<ImageView
android:id="@+id/appIconIV"
android:src="@drawable/alpha"
android:layout_width="60dp"
android:layout_height="60dp" />

<TextView
android:id="@+id/aNametxt"
android:text="Android Name"
android:textSize="20sp"
android:layout_marginTop="8dp"
android:maxLines="1"
android:layout_width="match_parent"
android:layout_height="wrap_content"
android:layout_alignParentTop="true"
android:layout_toRightOf="@+id/appIconIV"
android:layout_toEndOf="@+id/appIconIV"
android:layout_marginLeft="12dp"
android:layout_marginStart="12dp" />

<TextView
android:id="@+id/aVersiontxt"
android:text="Android Version"
android:textSize="14sp"
android:maxLines="1"
android:layout_width="match_parent"
android:layout_height="wrap_content"
android:layout_below="@+id/aNametxt"
android:layout_alignLeft="@+id/aNametxt"
android:layout_alignStart="@+id/aNametxt" />

</RelativeLayout>
```

– Now we need an adapter to populate the ListView.
– Right click on package folder i.e in my case in.ajitvoice.customlistviewexample, New and then click on java class.

– Name the class as ListAdapter and extend it with BaseAdapter.
– Now create a constructor for the class and all overriding methods as given below.

ListAdapter.java file:
package in.ajitvoice.customlistviewexample;

```java
import android.content.Context;
import android.support.annotation.NonNull;
import android.support.annotation.Nullable;
import android.view.LayoutInflater;
import android.view.View;
import android.view.ViewGroup;
import android.widget.ArrayAdapter;
import android.widget.BaseAdapter;
import android.widget.ImageView;
import android.widget.TextView;
import java.util.ArrayList;

public class ListAdapter extends BaseAdapter {

    Context context;
    private final String [] values;
    private final String [] numbers;
    private final int [] images;

    public ListAdapter(Context context, String [] values, String [] numbers, int [] images){
        //super(context, R.layout.single_list_app_item, utilsArrayList);
        this.context = context;
        this.values = values;
        this.numbers = numbers;
        this.images = images;
    }

    @Override
    public int getCount() {
        return values.length;
    }
```

```java
@Override
public Object getItem(int i) {
    return i;
}

@Override
public long getItemId(int i) {
    return i;
}

@NonNull
@Override
public View getView(int position, @Nullable View convertView, @NonNull ViewGroup parent) {
    ViewHolder viewHolder;

    final View result;

    if (convertView == null) {
        viewHolder = new ViewHolder();
        LayoutInflater inflater = LayoutInflater.from(context);
        convertView = inflater.inflate(R.layout.single_list_item, parent, false);
        viewHolder.txtName = (TextView) convertView.findViewById(R.id.aNametxt);
        viewHolder.txtVersion=(TextView) convertView.findViewById(R.id.aVersiontxt);
        viewHolder.icon = (ImageView) convertView.findViewById(R.id.appIconIV);
        result=convertView;
        convertView.setTag(viewHolder);
    } else {
        viewHolder = (ViewHolder) convertView.getTag();
        result=convertView;
    }

    viewHolder.txtName.setText(values[position]);
    viewHolder.txtVersion.setText("Version: "+numbers[position]);
    viewHolder.icon.setImageResource(images[position]);

    return convertView;
}
```

```
    private static class ViewHolder {
        TextView txtName;
        TextView txtVersion;
        ImageView icon;
    }
}
```

– Final step is to create array for Images and Text to be populated into ListView. Also connect the ListView component in layout file and setup the adapter in our MainActivity.

MainActivity.java file:
package in.ajitvoice.customlistviewexample;

import android.support.v7.app.AppCompatActivity;
import android.os.Bundle;
import android.view.View;
import android.widget.AdapterView;
import android.widget.ListView;
import android.widget.Toast;

public class MainActivity extends AppCompatActivity {

int[ ] images = {R.drawable.alpha, R.drawable.beta, R.drawable.cupcake,
R.drawable.donut, R.drawable.eclair, R.drawable.froyo, R.drawable.gingerbread,
R.drawable.honeycomb, R.drawable.icecreamsandwich, R.drawable.jellybean,
R.drawable.kitkat, R.drawable.lollipop, R.drawable.marshmallow, R.drawable.nougat};

String[ ] version = {"Android Alpha", "Android Beta", "Android Cupcake", "Android
Donut", "Android Eclair", "Android Froyo", "Android Gingerbread", "Android
Honeycomb", "Android Ice Cream Sandwich", "Android JellyBean", "Android Kitkat",
"Android Lollipop", "Android Marshmallow", "Android Nougat"};

String[ ] versionNumber = {"1.0", "1.1", "1.5", "1.6", "2.0", "2.2", "2.3", "3.0", "4.0", "4.1",
"4.4", "5.0", "6.0", "7.0"};

```java
ListView lView;
ListAdapter lAdapter;

@Override
protected void onCreate(Bundle savedInstanceState) {
    super.onCreate(savedInstanceState);
    setContentView(R.layout.activity_main);

    lView = (ListView) findViewById(R.id.androidList);

    lAdapter = new ListAdapter(MainActivity.this, version, versionNumber, images);

    lView.setAdapter(lAdapter);

    lView.setOnItemClickListener(new AdapterView.OnItemClickListener() {
        @Override
        public void onItemClick(AdapterView<?> adapterView, View view, int i, long l) {

            Toast.makeText(MainActivity.this,        version[i]+"        "+versionNumber[i],
Toast.LENGTH_SHORT).show();
        }
    });

    }
}
```

– Run the code to see the results.

Android GridView

In android, Grid View is a ViewGroup that is used to display items in a two dimensional, scrollable grid and grid items are automatically inserted to the gridview layout using a list adapter.

Generally, the adapter pulls data from sources such as an array or database and converts each item into a result view and that's placed into the list.

Following is the pictorial representation of GridView in android applications.

Picture - 12q

Following is the simple example showing user details using GridView and showing the position of a particular image when clicking on it in android applications.

Create a new android application using android studio and give names as GridView. In case if you are not aware of creating an app in android studio check this article Android Hello World App.

Once we create an application, add some sample images to project /res/drawable directory to show the images in GridView.

Now open an activity_main.xml file from /res/layout path and write the code like as shown below:

activity_main.xml

```xml
<?xml version="1.0" encoding="utf-8"?>
<GridView xmlns:android="http://schemas.android.com/apk/res/android"
    android:id="@+id/gridview"
    android:layout_width="match_parent"
    android:layout_height="match_parent"
    android:columnWidth="110dp"
    android:numColumns="auto_fit"
    android:verticalSpacing="10dp"
    android:horizontalSpacing="10dp"
    android:stretchMode="columnWidth"
    android:gravity="center" />
```

Once we are done with creation of layout, we need to create a custom adapter (ImageAdapter.java) by extending it using BaseExtender to show all the items in the grid, for that right click on java folder à Give name as ImageAdapter.java and click OK.

Open ImageAdapter.java file and write the code like as shown below

ImageAdapter.java

```java
package in.ajitvoice.gridview;
import android.content.Context;
import android.view.View;
import android.view.ViewGroup;
import android.widget.BaseAdapter;
import android.widget.GridView;
import android.widget.ImageView;

public class ImageAdapter extends BaseAdapter {
    private Context mContext;
    public ImageAdapter(Context c) {
        mContext = c;
    }
    public int getCount() {
        return thumbImages.length;
    }
    public Object getItem(int position) {
        return null;
```

```
    }
    public long getItemId(int position) {
       return 0;
    }
    // create a new ImageView for each item referenced by the Adapter
    public View getView(int position, View convertView, ViewGroup parent) {
        ImageView imageView = new ImageView(mContext);
        imageView.setLayoutParams(new GridView.LayoutParams(200, 200));
        imageView.setScaleType(ImageView.ScaleType.CENTER_CROP);
        imageView.setPadding(8, 8, 8, 8);
        imageView.setImageResource(thumbImages[position]);
        return imageView;
    }
    // Add all our images to arraylist
    public Integer[] thumbImages = {
        R.drawable.img1, R.drawable.img2,
        R.drawable.img3, R.drawable.img4,
        R.drawable.img5, R.drawable.img6,
        R.drawable.img7, R.drawable.img8,
        R.drawable.img1, R.drawable.img2,
        R.drawable.img3, R.drawable.img4,
        R.drawable.img5, R.drawable.img6,
        R.drawable.img7, R.drawable.img8,
        R.drawable.img1, R.drawable.img2,
        R.drawable.img3, R.drawable.img4,
        R.drawable.img5
    };
}
```

If you observe above code we referred some images, actually those are the sample images which we added in /res/drawable directory.

Now, we will bind images to our GridView using our custom adapter (ImageAdapter.java), for that open main activity file MainActivity.java from \java\in.ajitvoice.gridview path and write the code like as shown below.

MainActivity.java

```java
package in.ajitvoice.gridview;
import android.support.v7.app.AppCompatActivity;
import android.os.Bundle;
import android.view.View;
import android.widget.AdapterView;
import android.widget.GridView;
import android.widget.Toast;

public class MainActivity extends AppCompatActivity {
    @Override
    protected void onCreate(Bundle savedInstanceState) {
        super.onCreate(savedInstanceState);
        setContentView(R.layout.activity_main);
        GridView gv = (GridView) findViewById(R.id.gvDetails);
        gv.setAdapter(new ImageAdapter(this));
        gv.setOnItemClickListener(new AdapterView.OnItemClickListener() {
            public void onItemClick(AdapterView<?> parent, View v, int position, long id) {
                Toast.makeText(MainActivity.this, "Image Position: " + position,
Toast.LENGTH_SHORT).show();
            }
        });
    }
}
```

If you observe above code, we are binding image details to GridView using our custom adapter (ImageAdapter.java) and calling our layout using setContentView method in the form of R.layout.layout_file_name. Here our xml file name is activity_main.xml so we used file name activity_main.

Generally, during the launch of our activity, onCreate() callback method will be called by android framework to get the required layout for an activity.

When we run above example using the android virtual device (AVD) we will get a result like as shown below.

Picture-12r

This is how we can bind images to GridView using Adapter in android applications based on our requirements.

Android Styles and Themes

In android, Styles and Themes are used to change the look and feel of Views and appearance of application based on our requirements. By using Styles and Themes we can reduce the code duplication and make our app light & responsive.

Generally, the style is a combination of multiple attributes such as background color, font color, font size, font style, height, width, padding, margin, etc. and it is used to change the look and feel of View or window.

Styles in Android allow you to define the look and feel, for example colors and fonts, of Android components in XML resource files. This way you have to set common style attributes only once in one central place.

This is typically used for reducing styling duplication in a way highly analogous to CSS in the web development world. By specifying styles in one central file, we can then apply consistent styling across our application's views.

In android, the style is defined in a separate XML resource file and we can use that defined style for the Views in XML that specifies the layout. The Styles in android are similar to CSS styles in web design.

Defining and Using Styles

First, you define the XML style in res/values/styles.xml:
```
<resources>
<style name="LargeRedFont">
  <item name="android:textColor">#C80000</item>
  <item name="android:textSize">40sp</item>
</style>
</resources>
```

Now you can use the style within your activities in Main_Activity.xml:
```
<TextView
  android:id="@+id/tv_text"
  style="@style/LargeRedFont"
  android:layout_width="wrap_content"
```

```
android:layout_height="wrap_content"
android:text="@string/hello_world" />
```

Inheriting Styles

In many cases, you may want to extend a style and modify certain attributes. The parent attribute in the <style> element lets you specify a style from which your style should inherit properties. You can use this to inherit properties from an existing style and then define only the properties that you want to change or add.

```
<style name="LargeFont">
  <item name="android:textSize">40sp</item>
</style>

<style name="LargeBlueFont" parent="@style/LargeFont">
 <item name="android:textColor">#00007f</item>
</style>

<style name="CustomButton" parent="@android:style/Widget.Button">
 <item name="android:gravity">center_vertical|center_horizontal</item>
 <item name="android:textColor">#FFFFFF</item>
</style>
```

If you want to inherit from styles that you've defined yourself, you do not even have to use the parent attribute. Instead, as a shortcut just prefix the name of the style you want to inherit to the name of your new style, separated by a period:

```
<style name="LargeFont">
  <item name="android:textSize">40sp</item>
</style>

<style name="LargeFont.Red">
  <item name="android:textColor">#C80000</item>
</style>
```

Red is a child style and LargeFont is a parent style.

You can continue to extend styles inheriting from them by using multiple periods:

```
<style name="LargeFont.Red.Bold">
  <item name="android:textStyle">bold</item>
</style>

<style name="LargeFont.Red.Big">
  <item name="android:textSize">30sp</item>
</style>
```

Note: You can't inherit Android built-in styles this way. To reference a built-in style you must use the parent attribute:

```
<style name="CustomButton" parent="@android:style/Widget.Button">
 <item name="android:gravity">center_vertical|center_horizontal</item>
 <item name="android:textColor">#FFFFFF</item>
</style>
```

Using Themes

In some cases, we want to apply a consistent theme to all activities within our application. Instead of applying the style to a particular individual view, you can apply a collection of styles as a Theme to an Activity or application. When you do so, every View within the Activity or application will apply each property that it supports.

Defining a Theme

In android, theme is a style that is applied to an entire activity or app, instead of an individual View like as mentioned above. When we applied a style as a theme, the views in activity or app apply to the all style attributes that supports. For example. If we apply TextviewStyle as a theme for an activity, then the text of all the views in activity appears in the same style.

Following is the example of defining a theme in the android application.

```
<color name="custom_theme_color">#b0b0ff</color>
<style name="CustomTheme" parent="Theme.AppCompat.Light">
  <item name="android:windowBackground">@color/custom_theme_color</item>
  <item name="android:colorBackground">@color/custom_theme_color</item>
</style>
```

The above code overrides windowBackground and colorBackground properties of Theme.AppCompat.Light theme. To set a theme for a particular activity, open AndroidManifest.xml file and write the code like as shown below:

<activity android:theme="@android:style/CustomTheme">

In case, if we want to set the theme for all the activities in android application, open AndroidManifest.xml file and write the code like as shown below:

<application android:theme="@android:style/CustomTheme">

Menu

In android, Menu is a part of the user interface (UI) component which is used to handle some common functionality around the application. By using Menus in our applications, we can provide better and consistent user experience throughout the application. We can use Menu APIs to represent user actions and other options in our android application activities.

Types of Menus

In android, we have a three fundamental type of Menus available to define a set of options and actions in our android applications. The following are the commonly used Menus in android applications.
- **Options Menu**
- **Context Menu**
- **Popup Menu**

Android Options Menu

In android, Options Menu is a primary collection of menu items for an activity and it is useful to implement actions that have a global impact on the app, such as Settings, Search, etc.

Figure-12s

Android Context Menu

In android, Context Menu is a floating menu that appears when the user performs a long click on an element and it is useful to implement actions that affect the selected content or context frame.

Figure-12s

Android Popup Menu

In android, Popup Menu displays a list of items in a vertical list that's anchored to the view that invoked the menu and it's useful for providing an overflow of actions that related to specific content.

Figure-12t

Define an Android Menu in XML File

For all menu types, Android provides a standard XML format to define menu items. Instead of building a menu in our activity's code, we should define a menu and all its items in an XML menu resource and load menu resource as a Menu object in our activity or fragment.

In android, to define menu, we need to create a new folder menu inside of our project resource directory (res/menu/) and add a new XML file to build the menu with the following elements.

- <menu> - It's a root element to define a Menu in XML file and it will hold one or more and elements.
- <item> - It is used to create a menu item and it represents a single item on the menu. This element may contain a nested <menu> element in order to create a submenu.
- <group> - It's an optional and invisible for <item> elements. It is used to categorize the menu items so they share properties such as active state and visibility.

Following is the example of defining a menu in an XML file (menu_example.xml).

```xml
<?xml version="1.0" encoding="utf-8"?>
<menu xmlns:android="http://schemas.android.com/apk/res/android">
  <item android:id="@+id/mail"
    android:icon="@drawable/ic_mail"
    android:title="@string/mail" />
  <item android:id="@+id/upload"
    android:icon="@drawable/ic_upload"
    android:title="@string/upload"
    android:showAsAction="ifRoom" />
  <item android:id="@+id/share"
    android:icon="@drawable/ic_share"
    android:title="@string/share" />
</menu>
```

The <item> element in menu supports different type of attributes to define item's behaviour and appearance. Following are the some of commonly used <item> attributes in android applications.

- android: id - It is used to uniquely identify an element in the application.
- android:icon - It is used to set the item's icon from drawable folder.
- android: title - It is used to set the item's title
- android:showAsAction - It is used to specify how the item should appear as an action item in the app bar.

In case if we want to add submenu in menu item, then we need to add a <menu> element as the child of an <item>. Following is the example of defining a submenu in menu item.

```xml
<?xml version="1.0" encoding="utf-8"?>
<menu xmlns:android="http://schemas.android.com/apk/res/android">
  <item android:id="@+id/file"
    android:title="@string/file" >
    <!-- "file" submenu -->
    <menu>
      <item android:id="@+id/create_new"
        android:title="@string/create_new" />
      <item android:id="@+id/open"
        android:title="@string/open" />
    </menu>
  </item>
</menu>
```

Register Android (Context) Menu from an Activity

```
public class MainActivity extends AppCompatActivity {
    Button btn;
    String contacts[ ]={"Ajay","Sachin","Sumit","Tarun","Yogesh"};
    @Override
    protected void onCreate(Bundle savedInstanceState) {
        super.onCreate(savedInstanceState);
        setContentView(R.layout.activity_main);
        btn=(Button)findViewById(R.id.button1);
        registerForContextMenu(btn);
}
```

Load Android (Context) Menu from an Activity

Once we are done with creation of menu, we need to load the menu resource from our activity using MenuInflater.inflate() like as shown below.

```
@Override
public void onCreateContextMenu(ContextMenu menu, View v, ContextMenuInfo menuInfo) {
    super.onCreateContextMenu(menu, v, menuInfo);
    MenuInflater inflater = getMenuInflater();
    inflater.inflate(R.menu.menu_example, menu);
}
```

If you observe above code we are calling our menu using MenuInflater.inflate() method in the form of R.menu.menu_file_name. Here our xml file name is menu_example.xml so we used file name menu_example.

Handle Android Context Menu Click Events

In android, we can handle a menu item click events using ItemSelected() event based on the menu type. Following is the example of handling a context menu item click event using onContextItemSelected().

```
@Override
public boolean onContextItemSelected(MenuItem item) {
```

```
switch (item.getItemId()) {
    case R.id.mail:
        // do something
        return true;
    case R.id.share:
        // do something
        return true;
    default:
        return super.onContextItemSelected(item);
}}
```

If you observe above code, the getItemId() method will get the id of selected menu item based on that we can perform our actions.

Option Menu

In android, Options Menu is a primary collection of menu items for an activity and it is useful to implement actions that have a global impact on the app, such as Settings, Search, etc.

Load Android Options Menu from an Activity

To specify the options menu for an activity, we need to override onCreateOptionsMenu() method and load the defined menu resource using MenuInflater.inflate() like as shown below.

```
@Override
public void onCreateOptionsMenu(ContextMenu menu, View v, ContextMenuInfo menuInfo)
{
    super.onCreateContextMenu(menu, v, menuInfo);
    MenuInflater inflater = getMenuInflater();
    inflater.inflate(R.menu.menu_example, menu);
}
```

Handle Android Options Menu Click Events

In android, we can handle options menu item click events using the onOptionsItemSelected() event method. Following is the example of handling a options menu item click event using onOptionsItemSelected().

```java
@Override
public boolean onOptionsItemSelected(MenuItem item) {
    switch (item.getItemId()) {
        case R.id.mail:
            // do something
            return true;
        case R.id.share:
            // do something
            return true;
        default:
            return super.onContextItemSelected(item);
    }}
```

Playing Media (MP3)

You need to put your .mp3 file in /res/raw for this to work! (Just create a new folder named "raw" in /res). Store/Put a file peace.mp3 (any other audio file) in it. Write this in your OnCreate() in your MainActivity:

```java
package in.ajitvoice.musicplayer;
import androidx.appcompat.app.AppCompatActivity;
import android.media.MediaPlayer;
import android.os.Bundle;
import android.widget.Button;
public class MainActivity extends AppCompatActivity {
    Button play, pause, exit;
    @Override
    protected void onCreate(Bundle savedInstanceState) {
        super.onCreate(savedInstanceState);
        setContentView(R.layout.activity_main);

        play = findViewById(R.id.play); // There are Three Buttons on the Activity
        pause = findViewById(R.id.pause);
        exit = findViewById(R.id.exit);

        MediaPlayer mediaPlayer = MediaPlayer.create(this, R.raw.peace);
        // Play Music
        play.setOnClickListener(v -> {
            mediaPlayer.start();
```

```java
        });

        // Pause Music
        pause.setOnClickListener(v -> {
            mediaPlayer.pause();
        });

        // Exit from app
        exit.setOnClickListener(v -> {
            finish();
            System.exit(0);
        });
    }
}
```

CHAPTER - 13

Designing User Interfaces with Layouts

Layout controls determine how and where on the screen child controls are drawn. Each type of layout control draws its children using particular rules. For instance, the LinearLayoutcontrol draws its child controls in a single horizontal row or a single vertical column. Similarly, a TableLayout control displays each child control in tabular format (in cells within specific rows and columns).

Application user interfaces can be simple or complex, involving many different screens or only a few. Layouts and user interface controls can be defined as application resources or created programmatically at runtime.

Android Measurement Unit & Densities

Android provide specific units of measurement, you should be aware of them at the time of giving size of an element on an Android UI.

- dp - Density-independent pixel. 160dp is equivalent to one inch of physical screen size. This is the recommended unit of measurement when specifying the dimension of views. The 160 dpi screen is the baseline density assumed by Android. You can specify either "dp" or "dip" when referring to a density-independent pixel.

- sp - Scale-independent pixel. This is similar to dp and is recommended for specifying font sizes.

- pt - Point. A point is defined to be 1/72 of an inch, based on the physical screen size.

- px - Pixel. Corresponds to actual pixels on the screen.

- mm - Millimeters - based on the physical size of the screen.

- in - Inches, based on the physical size of the screen.1 Inch OR 2.54 centimeters

Android has a set of six generalized densities:

- ldpi (low) ~120dpi

- mdpi (medium) ~160dpi

- hdpi (high) ~240dpi

- xhdpi (extra-high) ~320dpi

- xxhdpi (extra-extra-high) ~480dpi

- xxxhdpi (extra-extra-extra-high) ~640dpi

Android View Group

A View Group is a subclass of the View Class and can be considered as a super class of Layouts. It provides an invisible container to hold the views or layouts. ViewGroup instances and views work together as a container for Layouts. To understand in simpler words it can be understood as a special view that can hold other views that are often known as a child view.

Creating Layouts Using XML Resources

You can configure almost any ViewGroup or View (or View subclass) attribute using the XML layout resource files. This method greatly simplifies the user interface design process,moving much of the static creation and layout of user interface controls, and basic definition of control attributes, to the XML, instead of littering the code. Developers reserve the ability to alter these layouts programmatically as necessary, but they can set all the defaults in the XML template. You will recognize the following as a simple layout file with a LinearLayout and a single TextView control.

```
<?xml version="1.0" encoding="utf-8"?>

<LinearLayoutxmlns:android="http://schemas.android.com/apk/res/android"
        android:orientation="vertical"
        android:layout_width="fill_parent" android:layout_height="fill_parent" >
<TextView
        android:layout_width="fill_parent" android:layout_height="wrap_content"
        android:text="@string/hello" />
</LinearLayout>
```

This block of XML shows a basic layout with a single TextView. The first line, which you might recognize from most XML files, is required.

Creating only an XML file, though, won't actually draw anything on the screen. A particular layout is usually associated with a particular Activity. In your default Android project, there is only one activity, which sets the main.xml layout by default. To associate the main.xml layout with the activity, use the method call setContentView() with the identifier of the main.xml layout. The ID of the layout matches the XML filename without the extension. In this case, the preceding example came from main.xml, so the identifier of this layout is simply main:

```
setContentView(R.layout.main);
```

Layouts Programmatically

You can create user interface components such as layouts at runtime programmatically, but for organization and maintainability, it's best that you leave this for the odd case rather than the norm. The main reason is because the creation of layouts programmatically difficult to maintain, whereas the XML resource method is visual, more organized,and could be done by a separate designer with no Java skills.

The following example shows how to programmatically have an Activity instantiate a LinearLayout view and place two TextView objects within it. No resources whatsoever are used; actions are done at runtime instead.

```
public void onCreate(Bundle savedInstanceState)
{
        super.onCreate(savedInstanceState);
        TextView text1 = new TextView(this); text1.setText("Hi there!");
        TextView text2 = new TextView(this); text2.setText("I'm second. I need to
        wrap."); text2.setTextSize((float) 60);
        LinearLayoutll = new LinearLayout(this);
        ll.setOrientation(LinearLayout.VERTICAL); ll.addView(text1);
        ll.addView(text2); setContentView(ll);
}
```

The onCreate() method is called when the Activity is created. The first thing this method does is some normal Activity housekeeping by calling the constructor for the base class. Next, two TextView controls are instantiated. The Text property of each TextView is set using the setText() method. All TextView attributes, such as TextSize, are set by making method calls on the TextView object.These actions perform the same function that you have in the past by setting the properties Text and TextSize using the layout resource designer, except these properties are set at runtime instead of defined in the layout files compiled into your application package.

Built in layouts

The types of layouts built-in to the Android SDK framework include:

- FrameLayout
- Constraint Layout (Default)
- LinearLayout
- RelativeLayout
- TableLayout

All layouts, regardless of their type, have basic layout attributes. Layout attributes apply to any child View within that layout.You can set layout attributes at runtime programmatically, but ideally you set them in the XML layout files using the following syntax: android:layout_attribute_name="value"

There are several layout attributes that all ViewGroup objects share. These include size attributes and margin attributes. You can find basic layout attributes in the ViewGroup. LayoutParamsclass. The margin attributes enable each child View within a layout to have padding on each side. Find these attributes in the ViewGroup.MarginLayoutParams classes.There are also a number of ViewGroup attributes for handling child View drawing bounds and animation settings.

Frame Layout

You can, however, add multiple children to a FrameLayout and control their position within the FrameLayout by assigning gravity to each child, using the android:layout_gravity attribute.

Child views are drawn in a stack, with the most recently added child on top. The size of the FrameLayout is the size of its largest child (plus padding), visible or not (if the FrameLayout's parent permits). Views that are View. GONE are used for sizing only if setConsiderGoneChildrenWhenMeasuring() is set to true.

Following Table describes some of the important attributes specific to FrameLayout views.

Attribute Name	Applies To	Description	Value
android: foreground	Parent view	Drawable to draw over the content	Drawable resource.
android: foreground-Gravity	Parent view	Gravity of foreground drawable.	One or more constants separated by "|". The constants available are top, bottom, left, right, center_vertical, fill_vertical, center_horizontal, fill_horizontal, center, and fill.

android: measureAll-Children	Parent view	Restrict size of layout to all child views or just the child views set to VISIBLE (and not those set to INVISIBLE).	True or false.
android: layout_ gravity	Child view	A gravity constant that describes how to place the child View within the parent.	One or more constants separated by "|". The constants available are top, bottom, left, right, center_vertical, fill_ vertical, center_horizontal, fill_horizontal, center, and fill.

Table-21

An Example of FlowLayout is shown below

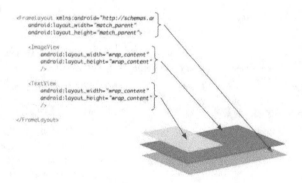

Figure-13a

LinearLayout

A LinearLayout view organizes its child View objects in a single row or column, depending on whether its orientation attribute is set to horizontal or vertical. This is a very handy layout method for creating forms.

You can find the layout attributes available for LinearLayout child View objects in android.control.LinearLayout.LayoutParams. Following table describes some of the important attributes specific to LinearLayout views.

Attribute Name	Applies To	Description	Value
android: orientation	Parent view	Layout is a single row (horizontal) or single column (vertical).	Horizontal or Vertical
android: gravity	Parent view	Gravity of child views within layout.	One or more constants separated by"|". The constants available are top,bottom, left, right, center_vertical, fill_vertical, center_horizontal, fill_horizontal, center, and fill.
android: layout_ gravity	Child View	The gravity for a specific child view. Used for positioning of views.	One or more constants separated by"|". The constants available are top,bottom, left, right, center_vertical, fill_vertical, center_horizontal, fill_horizontal, center, and fill.
android: layout_ weight	Child view	The weight for a specific child view. Used to provide ratio of screen space used within the parent control.	The sum of values across all child views in a parent view must equal 1.For example, one child control might have a value of .3 and another have a value of .7.

Table-22

Constraint Layout

Constraint Layout (Default) is a ViewGroup (i.e. a view that holds other views) which allows you to create large and complex layouts with a flat view hierarchy, and also allows you to position and size widgets in a very flexible way. It was created to help reduce the nesting of views and also improve the performance of layout files.

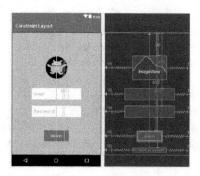

Figure-13c

ConstraintLayout is very similar to RelativeLayout in such a way because, views are laid out according to relationships between sibling views and the parent layout yet it's a lot more flexible and works better with the Layout Editor of the Android Studio's. It was released at Google I/O 2016. Since it came into existence, it has become a wildly used viewgroup and supports Android 2.3 or higher.

Important Note: To define a view's position in ConstraintLayout, you must add at least one horizontal and one vertical constraint to the view. Each constraint defines the view's position along either the vertical or horizontal axis; so each view must have a minimum of one constraint for each axis, but often more are necessary.

Advantages Of Constraint Layout Over Other Layouts

1. One great advantage of the constraintlayout is that you can perform animations on your ConstraintLayout views with very little code.
2. You can build your complete layout with simple drag-and-drop on the Android Studio design editor.
3. You can control what happens to a group of widgets through a single line of code.
4. Constraint Layout improve performance over other layout

Using Constraint Layout In Android Studio:

It is not bundled as part of Android SDK and is available as a support library. Due to this, any update in the future would be compatible with all versions of Android.

To use Constraint Layout make sure you have declared below repository in build.gradle file

```
repositories
{
  maven
  {
    url 'https://maven.google.com'
  }
}
```

Now to use ConstraintLayout features in our android project, we will need to add the library to our build.gradle app module dependencies section.
Open your build.gradle (Module app) and add the code below:
```
dependencies
{
  compile 'com.android.support.constraint:constraint-layout:1.1.0-beta3'
}
```

Relative Layout

The RelativeLayout view enables you to specify where the child view controls are in relation to each other. For instance, you can set a child View to be positioned "above" or"below" or "to the left of " or "to the right of " another View, referred to by its unique identifier. You can also align child View objects relative to one another or the parent layout edges. Combining RelativeLayout attributes can simplify creating interesting user interfaces without resorting to multiple layout groups to achieve a desired effect. You can find the layout attributes available for RelativeLayout child View objects in android.control.RelativeLayout.LayoutParams. Following Table describes some of the important attributes specific to RelativeLayout views.

Attribute Name	Applies To	Description	Value
android:gravity	Parent view	Gravity of child views within layout.	One or more constants separa ted by "|". The constants available are top, bottom,left, right,center_verti cal,fill_vertical,ce nter_horizontal,fi ll_horizontal,cent er, and fill.
android: layout_centerInParent	Child view	Centers child view horizontally and vertically within parent view.	True or False
android: layout_centerHorizont al	Child view	Centers child view horizontally within parent view	True or False
android: layout_centerVertical	Child view	Centers child view vertically within parent view.	True or False

61

android: layout_alignParentTop	Child view	Aligns child view with top edge of parent view	True or False
android: layout_alignParentBot t om	Child view	Aligns child view with bottomedge of parent view.	True or False
android: layout_alignParentLe ft	Child View	Aligns child view with leftedge of parent view.	True or False
android: layout_alignParentRi gh t	Child View	Aligns child view with rightedge of parent view.	True or False
android: layout_alignRight	Child View	Aligns child view with rightedge of another child view,specified by ID.	A view ID; for example, @id/Button1
android: layout_alignLeft	Child View	Aligns child view with leftedge of another child view,specified by ID.	A view ID; for example, @id/Button1
android: layout_alignTop	Child View	A view ID; for example, @id/Button1	
android: layout_alignBottom	Child View	A view ID; for example, @id/Button1	
android: layout_above	Child View	Positions bottom edge of child view above another child view, specified by ID.	A view ID; for example, @id/Button1
android: layout_below	Child View	Positions top edge of childview below another childview, specified by ID.	A view ID; for example, @id/Button1

android: layout_toLeftOf	Child View	Positions right edge of childview to the left of another child view, specified by ID.	A view ID; for example, @id/Button1
android: layout_toRightOf	Child View	Positions left edge of childview to the right of another child view, specified by ID.	A view ID; for example, @id/Button1

Table-23

Following figure shows how each of the button controls is relative to each other.

Figure-13d

Here's an example of an XML layout resource with a RelativeLayout and two child View objects, a Button object aligned relative to its parent, and an ImageView aligned and positioned relative to the Button (and the parent):

```
<?xml version="1.0" encoding="utf-8"?>

<RelativeLayoutxmlns:android="http://schemas.android.com/apk/res/android"
        android:id="@+id/RelativeLayout01"   android:layout_height="fill_parent"
        android:layout_width="fill_parent">

    <Buttonandroid:id="@+id/ButtonCenter" android:text="Center"
            android:layout_width="wrap_content" android:layout_height="
            wrap_content" android:layout_centerInParent="true" />
    <ImageViewandroid:id="@+id/ImageView01" android:layout_width="
```

63

```
            wrap_content" android:layout_height="wrap_content"
            android:layout_above="@id/ButtonCenter"
            android:layout_centerHorizontal="true" android:src="
            @drawable/arrow" />
</RelativeLayout>
```

TableLayout

A TableLayout view organizes children into rows, as shown in following Figure-13e. You add individual View objects within each row of the table using a TableRow layout View (which is basically a horizontally oriented LinearLayout) for each row of the table. Each column of the TableRow can contain one View (or layout with child View objects). You place ViewItems added to a TableRow in columns in the order they are added.You can specify the column number (zero-based) to skip columns as necessary ; otherwise, the View object is put in the next column to the right. Columns scale to the size of the largest View of that column. You can also include normal View objects instead of TableRow elements, if you want the View to take up an entire row. You can find the layout attributes available for TableLayout child View objects in android.control.TableLayout.LayoutParams. You can find the layout attributes available for TableRow child View objects in android.control.TableRow.LayoutParams.

Following Table describes some of the important attributes specific to TableLayout View objects.

Attribute Name	Applies To	Description	Value
android:collapseColumns	TableLayout	A comma-delimited list of column indices to collapse (0-based)	String or string resource. For example, "0,1,3,5"
android: shrinkColumns	TableLayout	A comma-delimited list of column indices to shrink (0-based)	String or string resource.Use "*" for all columns. For example, "0,1,3,5"
andriod: stretchColumns	TableLayout	A comma-delimited list of column indices to stretch (0-based)	String or string resource.Use "*" for all columns. For example, "0,1,3,5"
android: layout_column	TableRow child view	Index of column this child view should be displayed in (0-based)	Integer or integer resource. For example, 1
android: layout_span	TableRow child view	Number of columns this child view should span across	Integer or integer resource greater than or equal to 1. For example, 3

Table-24

65

Here's an example of an XML layout resource with a TableLayout with two rows (two TableRow child objects). The TableLayout is set to stretch the columns to the size of the screen width. The first TableRow has three columns; each cell has a Button object. The second TableRow puts only one Button view into the second column explicitly:

```
<TableLayoutxmlns:android="http://schemas.android.com/apk/res/android"
      android:id="@+id/TableLayout01"
      android:layout_width="fill_parent" android:layout_height="fill_parent"
      android:stretchColumns="*">
      <TableRowandroid:id="@+id/TableRow01">
      <Buttonandroid:id="@+id/ButtonLeft" android:text="Left Door" />
            <Buttonandroid:id="@+id/ButtonMiddle" android:text="Middle
                  Door" />
            <Buttonandroid:id="@+id/ButtonRight" android:text="Right Door" />
      </TableRow>

      <TableRowandroid:id="@+id/TableRow02">

            <Buttonandroid:id="@+id/ButtonBack" android:text="Go Back"
                  android:layout_column="1" />

      </TableRow>

</TableLayout>
```

Using Data-Driven Containers

Some of the View container controls are designed for displaying repetitive View objects ina particular way. Examples of this type of View container control include ListView, GridView, and GalleryView:

- ListView: Contains a vertically scrolling, horizontally filled list of View objects, each of which typically contains a row of data; the user can choose an item to perform some action upon.
- GridView: Contains a grid of View objects, with a specific number of columns; this container is often used with image icons; the user can choose an item to perform some action upon.
- GalleryView: Contains a horizontally scrolling list of View objects, also often used with image icons; the user can select an item to perform some action upon.

These containers are all types of AdapterView controls.An AdapterView control contains a set of child View controls to display data from some data source. An

66

Adapter generates these child View controls from a data source. As this is an important part of all these container controls, we talk about the Adapter objects first.

In this section, you learn how to bind data to View objects using Adapter objects. In the Android SDK, an Adapter reads data from some data source and provides a View object based on some rules, depending on the type of Adapter used. This View is used to populate the child View objects of a particular AdapterView.

The most common Adapter classes are the CursorAdapter and the ArrayAdapter. The CursorAdapter gathers data from a Cursor, whereas the ArrayAdapter gathers data from an array. A CursorAdapter is a good choice to use when using data from a database. The ArrayAdapter is a good choice to use when there is only a single column of data or when the data comes from a resource array.

When making an Adapter, refer to both the layout resource and the identifier of the TextView control. The Android SDK provides some common layout resources for use in your application.

How to Use the Adapter

An ArrayAdapter binds each element of the array to a single View object within the layout resource. Here is an example of creating an ArrayAdapter:

```
private String[ ] items = {"Item 1", "Item 2", "Item 3" };
ArrayAdapter adapt =new ArrayAdapter<String>(this, R.layout.textview, items);
```

In this example, we have a String array called items.This is the array used by the ArrayAdapter as the source data. We also use a layout resource, which is the View that is repeated for each item in the array. This is defined as follows:

```
<TextViewxmlns:android="http://schemas.android.com/apk/res/android"
android:layout_width="fill_parent" android:layout_height="wrap_content"
android:textSize="20px" />
```

This layout resource contains only a single TextView. However, you can use a more complex layout with the constructors that also take the resource identifier of a TextView within the layout. Each child View within the AdapterView that uses this Adapter gets one TextView instance with one of the strings from the String array.

If you have an array resource defined, you can also directly set the entries attribute for an AdapterView to the resource identifier of the array to automatically provide the ArrayAdapter.

How to use Cursor Adapter

A CursorAdapter binds one or more columns of data to one or more View objects within the layout resource provided. This is best shown with an example. The following example demonstrates creating a CursorAdapter by querying the Contacts contentprovider. The CursorAdapter requires the use of a Cursor.

```
Cursor names = managedQuery(Contacts.Phones.CONTENT_URI, null, null, null,
null);
startManagingCursor(names);

ListAdapter adapter = new SimpleCursorAdapter( this, R.layout.two_text,
    names, new String[ ]
    {
        Contacts.Phones.NAME, Contacts.Phones.NUMBER
    }, new int[ ]
    {
        R.id.scratch_text1, R.id.scratch_text2
    });
```

In this example, we present a couple of new concepts. First, you need to know that the Cursor must contain a field named _id. In this case, we know that the Contacts contentprovider does have this field. This field is used later when you handle the user selecting a particular item.

We make a call to managedQuery() to get the Cursor. Then, we instantiate a SimpleCursorAdapter as a ListAdapter. Our layout, R.layout.two_text, has two TextView objects in it, which are used in the last parameter. SimpleCursorAdapter enables us to match up columns in the database with particular controls in our layout. For each row returned from the query, we get one instance of the layout within our AdapterView.

Binding Data to the AdapterView

Now that you have an Adapter object, you can apply this to one of the AdapterView controls. Any of them works. Although the Gallery technically takes a SpinnerAdapter, the instantiation of SimpleCursorAdapter also returns a SpinnerAdapter. Here is an example of this with a ListView, continuing on from the previous sample code: ((ListView)findViewById(R.id.list)).

The call to the setAdapter() method of the AdapterView, a ListView in this case, should come after your call to setContentView(). This is all that is required to bind data to your AdapterView.

Handling Selection Events

You often use AdapterView controls to present data from which the user should select. All three of the discussed controls - ListView, GridView, and Gallery - enable your application to monitor for click events in the same way. You need to call setOnItemClickListener() on your AdapterView and pass in an implementation of the AdapterView.OnItemClickListener class.

Following is an example implementation of this class:

```
av.setOnItemClickListener
(
        new AdapterView.OnItemClickListener()
        {
        public void onItemClick(
                AdapterView<?> parent, View view, int position, long id)
```

```
            {
                  Toast.makeText(Scratch.this, "Clicked _id="+id,
                        Toast.LENGTH_SHORT).show();

            }

      });
```

In the preceding example, av is our AdapterView. The implementation of the onItemClick() method is where all the interesting work happens. The parent parameter is the AdapterView where the item was clicked. This is useful if your screen has more than one AdapterView on it. The View parameter is the specific View within the item that was clicked. The position is the zero-based position within the list of items that the user selects.

Finally, the id parameter is the value of the _id column for the particular item that the user selects. This is useful for querying for further information about that particular row of data that the item represents. Your application can also listen for long-click events on particular items. Additionally, your application can listen for selected items. Although the parameters are the same, your application receives a call as the highlighted item changes. This can be in response to the user scrolling with the arrow keys and not selecting an item for action.

Attributes of Layout in Android

The following are the attributes for customizing a Layout while defining it:
- android:id: It uniquely identifies the Android Layout.
- android:hint: It shows the hint of what to fill inside the EditText.
- android:layout_height: It sets the height of the layout.
- android:layout_width: It sets the width of the layout.
- android:layout_gravity: It sets the position of the child view.
- android:layout_marginTop: It sets the margin of the from the top of the layout.
- android:layout_marginBottom: It sets the margin of the from the bottom of the layout.
- android:layout_marginLeft: It sets the margin of the from the left of the layout.
- android:layout_marginRight: It sets the margin of the from the right of the layout.
- android:layout_x: It specifies the x coordinates of the layout.
- android:layout_y: It specifies the y coordinates of the layout.

70

ScrollView

In android, ScrollView is a kind of layout that is useful to add vertical or horizontal scroll bars to the content which is larger than the actual size of layouts such as linearlayout, relativelayout, framelayout, etc.

Generally, the android ScrollView is useful when we have content that doesn't fit our android app layout screen. The ScrollView will enable a scroll to the content which is exceeding the screen layout and allow users to see the complete content by scrolling.

The android ScrollView can hold only one direct child. In case, if we want to add multiple views within the scroll view, then we need to include them in another standard layout like linearlayout, relativelayout, framelayout, etc.

To enable scrolling for our android applications, ScrollView is the best option but we should not use ScrollView along with ListView or Gridview because they both will take care of their own vertical scrolling.

In android, ScrollView supports only vertical scrolling. In case, if we want to implement horizontal scrolling, then we need to use a HorizontalScrollView component. The android ScrollView is having a property called android:fillViewport, which is used to define whether the ScrollView should stretch it's content to fill the viewport or not.

Android ScrollView Example

Following is the example of enabling vertical scrolling to the content which is larger than the layout screen using an android ScrollView object.

Create a new android application using android studio and give names as MyScrollView.

Once we create an application, open activity_main.xml file from \res\layout folder path and write the code like as shown below.

activity_main.xml
<?xml version="1.0" encoding="utf-8"?>

```xml
<ScrollView xmlns:android="http://schemas.android.com/apk/res/android"
    android:layout_width="match_parent"
    android:layout_height="wrap_content"
    android:fillViewport="false">
<LinearLayout xmlns:android="http://schemas.android.com/apk/res/android"
    android:orientation="vertical" android:layout_width="match_parent"
    android:layout_height="match_parent">
    <TextView android:id="@+id/loginscrn"
        android:layout_width="wrap_content"
        android:layout_height="wrap_content"
        android:layout_marginTop="80dp"
        android:text="ScrollView"
        android:textSize="25dp"
        android:textStyle="bold"
        android:layout_gravity="center"/>
    <TextView android:id="@+id/fstTxt"
        android:layout_width="wrap_content"
        android:layout_height="wrap_content"
        android:layout_marginTop="20dp"
        android:text="Welcome to AjitVoice"
        android:layout_gravity="center"/>
    <Button android:layout_width="wrap_content"
        android:layout_height="wrap_content"
        android:layout_gravity="center"
        android:layout_marginTop="60dp"
        android:text="Button One" />
    <Button android:layout_width="wrap_content"
        android:layout_height="wrap_content"
        android:layout_gravity="center"
        android:layout_marginTop="60dp"
        android:text="Button Two" />
    <Button android:layout_width="wrap_content"
        android:layout_height="wrap_content"
        android:layout_gravity="center"
        android:layout_marginTop="60dp"
        android:text="Button Three" />
    <Button android:layout_width="wrap_content"
        android:layout_height="wrap_content"
        android:layout_gravity="center"
```

```
        android:layout_marginTop="60dp"
        android:text="Button Four" />
    <Button android:layout_width="wrap_content"
        android:layout_height="wrap_content"
        android:layout_gravity="center"
        android:layout_marginTop="60dp"
        android:text="Button Five" />
    <Button android:layout_width="wrap_content"
        android:layout_height="wrap_content"
        android:layout_gravity="center"
        android:layout_marginTop="60dp"
        android:text="Button Six" />
    <Button android:layout_width="wrap_content"
        android:layout_height="wrap_content"
        android:layout_gravity="center"
        android:layout_marginTop="60dp"
        android:text="Button Seven" />
    <Button android:layout_width="wrap_content"
        android:layout_height="wrap_content"
        android:layout_gravity="center"
        android:layout_marginTop="60dp"
        android:text="Button Eight" />
    <Button android:layout_width="wrap_content"
        android:layout_height="wrap_content"
        android:layout_gravity="center"
        android:layout_marginTop="60dp"
        android:text="Button Nine" />
</LinearLayout>
</ScrollView>
```

If you observe above code, we used a ScrollView to enable the scrolling for linearlayout whenever the content exceeds layout screen.

Android HorizontalScrollView

Open activity_main.xml file in your android application and write the code like as shown below.

activity_main.xml

```xml
<?xml version="1.0" encoding="utf-8"?>
<HorizontalScrollView
xmlns:android="http://schemas.android.com/apk/res/android"
    android:layout_width="match_parent"
    android:layout_height="wrap_content"
    android:fillViewport="true">
<LinearLayout xmlns:android="http://schemas.android.com/apk/res/android"
    android:orientation="horizontal" android:layout_width="match_parent"
    android:layout_height="match_parent"
    android:layout_marginTop="150dp">
    <Button android:layout_width="wrap_content"
        android:layout_height="wrap_content"
        android:text="Button One" />
    <Button android:layout_width="wrap_content"
        android:layout_height="wrap_content"
        android:text="Button Two" />
    <Button android:layout_width="wrap_content"
        android:layout_height="wrap_content"
        android:text="Button Three" />
    <Button android:layout_width="wrap_content"
        android:layout_height="wrap_content"
        android:text="Button Four" />
    <Button android:layout_width="wrap_content"
        android:layout_height="wrap_content"
        android:text="Button Five" />
    <Button android:layout_width="wrap_content"
        android:layout_height="wrap_content"
        android:text="Button Six" />
    <Button android:layout_width="wrap_content"
        android:layout_height="wrap_content"
        android:text="Button Seven" />
    <Button android:layout_width="wrap_content"
```

```
        android:layout_height="wrap_content"
        android:text="Button Eight" />
    <Button android:layout_width="wrap_content"
        android:layout_height="wrap_content"
        android:text="Button Nine" />
</LinearLayout>
</HorizontalScrollView>
```

If you observe above code, we used a HorizontalScrollView to enable horizontal scrolling for linearlayout whenever the content exceeds layout screen.

Shared Preferences

One of the most Interesting Data Storage options Android provides its users is Shared Preferences. Shared Preferences is the way in which one can store and retrieve small amounts of primitive data as key/value pairs to a file on the device storage such as String, int, float, Boolean that make up your preferences in an XML file inside the app on the device storage. Shared Preferences can be thought of as a dictionary or a key/value pair. For example, you might have a key being "username" and for the value, you might store the user's username. And then you could retrieve that by its key (here username). You can have a simple shared preference API that you can use to store preferences and pull them back as and when needed. Shared Preferences class provides APIs for reading, writing, and managing this data.

How to Create Shared Preferences?

The first thing we need to do is to create one shared preferences file per app. So name it with the package name of your app- unique and easy to associate with the app. When you want to get the values, call the getSharedPreferences() method. Shared Preferences provide modes of storing the data (private mode and public mode). It is for backward compatibility- use only MODE_PRIVATE to be secure.

public abstract SharedPreferences getSharedPreferences (String name, int mode)

This method takes two arguments, the first being the name of the SharedPreference(SP) file and the other is the context mode that we want to store our file in.

- MODE_PUBLIC will make the file public which could be accessible by other applications on the device

- MODE_PRIVATE keeps the files private and secures the user's data.

- MODE_APPEND is used while reading the data from the SP file.

Following is sample byte code on how to write Data in Shared Preferences:
// Storing data into SharedPreferences
SharedPreferences sharedPreferences =
getSharedPreferences("MySharedPref",MODE_PRIVATE);

76

```
// Creating an Editor object to edit(write to the file)
SharedPreferences.Editor myEdit = sharedPreferences.edit();

// Storing the key and its value as the data fetched from edittext
myEdit.putString("name", name.getText().toString());
myEdit.putInt("age", Integer.parseInt(age.getText().toString()));

// Once the changes have been made,
// we need to commit to apply those changes made,
// otherwise, it will throw an error
myEdit.commit();
```

Following is the sample byte code on how to read Data in Shared Preferences:
```
// Retrieving the value using its keys the file name
// must be same in both saving and retrieving the data
SharedPreferences sh = getSharedPreferences("MySharedPref", MODE_APPEND);

// The value will be default as empty string because for
// the very first time when the app is opened, there is nothing to show
String s1 = sh.getString("name", "");
int a = sh.getInt("age", 0);

// We can then use the data
name.setText(s1);
age.setText(String.valueOf(a));
```

Example to Demonstrate the use of Shared Preferences in Android
Below is the small demo for Shared Preferences. In this particular demo, there are two EditTexts, which save and retain the data entered earlier in them. This type of feature can be seen in applications with forms. Using Shared Preferences, the user will not have to fill in details again and again. Invoke the following code inside the activity_main.xml file to implement the UI:

```
<?xml version="1.0" encoding="utf-8"?>
<RelativeLayout
    xmlns:android="http://schemas.android.com/apk/res/android"
    xmlns:tools="http://schemas.android.com/tools"
    android:layout_width="match_parent"
```

```xml
    android:layout_height="match_parent"
    tools:context=".MainActivity"
    tools:ignore="HardcodedText">

    <TextView
        android:id="@+id/textview"
        android:layout_width="wrap_content"
        android:layout_height="wrap_content"
        android:layout_centerHorizontal="true"
        android:layout_marginTop="32dp"
        android:text="Shared Preferences Demo"
        android:textColor="@android:color/black"
        android:textSize="24sp" />

    <!--EditText to take the data from the user
        and save the data in SharedPreferences-->
    <EditText
        android:id="@+id/edit1"
        android:layout_width="match_parent"
        android:layout_height="wrap_content"
        android:layout_below="@+id/textview"
        android:layout_marginStart="16dp"
        android:layout_marginTop="8dp"
        android:layout_marginEnd="16dp"
        android:hint="Enter your Name"
        android:padding="10dp" />

    <!--EditText to take the data from the user and
        save the data in SharedPreferences-->
    <EditText
        android:id="@+id/edit2"
        android:layout_width="match_parent"
        android:layout_height="wrap_content"
        android:layout_below="@+id/edit1"
        android:layout_marginStart="16dp"
        android:layout_marginTop="8dp"
        android:layout_marginEnd="16dp"
        android:hint="Enter your Age"
```

```
      android:padding="10dp"
      android:inputType="number" />
```

```
</RelativeLayout>
```

Working with the MainActivity.java file to handle the two of the EditText to save the data entered by the user inside the SharedPreferences. Below is the code for the MainActivity.java file. Comments are added inside the code to understand the code in more detail.

```java
import androidx.appcompat.app.AppCompatActivity;
import android.content.SharedPreferences;
import android.os.Bundle;
import android.widget.EditText;

public class MainActivity extends AppCompatActivity {

    private EditText name, age;

    @Override
    protected void onCreate(Bundle savedInstanceState) {
        super.onCreate(savedInstanceState);
        setContentView(R.layout.activity_main);
        name = findViewById(R.id.edit1);
        age = findViewById(R.id.edit2);
    }

    // Fetch the stored data in onResume()
    // Because this is what will be called
    // when the app opens again
    @Override
    protected void onResume() {
        super.onResume();

        // Fetching the stored data
        // from the SharedPreference
        SharedPreferences sh = getSharedPreferences("MySharedPref",
MODE_PRIVATE);
```

```java
        String s1 = sh.getString("name", "");
        int a = sh.getInt("age", 0);

        // Setting the fetched data
        // in the EditTexts
        name.setText(s1);
        age.setText(String.valueOf(a));
    }

    // Store the data in the SharedPreference
    // in the onPause() method
    // When the user closes the application
    // onPause() will be called
    // and data will be stored
    @Override
    protected void onPause() {
        super.onPause();

        // Creating a shared pref object
        // with a file name "MySharedPref"
        // in private mode
        SharedPreferences sharedPreferences = getSharedPreferences("MySharedPref",
MODE_PRIVATE);
        SharedPreferences.Editor myEdit = sharedPreferences.edit();

        // write all the data entered by the user in SharedPreference and apply
        myEdit.putString("name", name.getText().toString());
        myEdit.putInt("age", Integer.parseInt(age.getText().toString()));
        myEdit.apply();
    }
}
```

CHAPTER - 14
Drawing and Working with Animation

Canvas and Paint

Components:
1. A Bitmap to hold the pixels,

2. A Canvas to host the draw calls (writing into the bitmap),

3. A drawing primitive (e.g. Rect, Path, text, Bitmap), and

4. A paint (to describe the colors and styles for the drawing).

The android.graphics framework divides drawing into two areas:

- What to draw, handled by Canvas.

- How to draw, handled by Paint.

For instance, Canvas provides a method to draw a line, while Paint provides methods to define that line's color. Canvas has a method to draw a rectangle, while Paint defines whether to fill that rectangle with a color or leave it empty. Simply put, Canvas defines shapes that you can draw on the screen, while Paint defines the color, style, font, and so forth of each shape you draw.

So, before you draw anything, you need to create one or more Paint objects. The PieChart example does this in a method called init, which is called from the constructor from Java.

```
private void init()
{
  textPaint = new Paint(Paint.ANTI_ALIAS_FLAG); textPaint.setColor(textColor);
  if (textHeight == 0) {
    textHeight = textPaint.getTextSize();
  } else
  {
    textPaint.setTextSize(textHeight);
  }
```

```
piePaint = new Paint(Paint.ANTI_ALIAS_FLAG);
piePaint.setStyle(Paint.Style.FILL); piePaint.setTextSize(textHeight);
shadowPaint = new Paint(0); shadowPaint.setColor(0xff101010);
shadowPaint.setMaskFilter(new BlurMaskFilter(8,
BlurMaskFilter.Blur.NORMAL));

    ...
```

Creating objects ahead of time is an important optimization. Views are redrawn very frequently, and many drawing objects require expensive initialization. Creating drawing objects within your onDraw() method significantly reduces performance and can make your UI appear sluggish.

Once you have your object creation and measuring code defined, you can implement onDraw(). Every view implements onDraw() differently, but there are some common operations that most views share:

- Draw text using drawText(). Specify the typeface by calling setTypeface(), and the text color by calling setColor().
- Draw primitive shapes using drawRect(), drawOval(), and drawArc(). Change whether the shapes are filled, outlined, or both by calling setStyle().
- Draw more complex shapes using the Path class. Define a shape by adding lines and curves to a Path object, then draw the shape using drawPath(). Just as with primitive shapes, paths can be outlined, filled, or both, depending on the setStyle().
- Define gradient fills by creating LinearGradient objects. Call setShader() to use your LinearGradient on filled shapes.
- Draw bitmaps using drawBitmap().

For example, here's the code that draws PieChart. It uses a mix of text, lines, and shapes.

```
protected void onDraw(Canvas canvas)
{
super.onDraw(canvas);
    // Draw the shadow canvas.drawOval(shadowBounds,shadowPaint);
    // Draw the label text
```

```
canvas.drawText(data.get(currentItem).mLabel, textX, textY, textPaint);
// Draw the pie slices

for (int i = 0; i<data.size(); ++i)

{

Item it = data.get(i); piePaint.setShader(it.shader);
    canvas.drawArc(bounds,360 - it.endAngle, it.endAngle - it.startAngle, true,
piePaint);
    }

    // Draw the pointer

canvas.drawLine(textX, pointerY, pointerX, pointerY, textPaint);
canvas.drawCircle(pointerX, pointerY, pointerSize, mTextPaint);
}
```

Bitmaps

You can find lots of goodies for working with graphics such as bitmaps in the android.graphics package. The core class for bitmaps is android.graphics. Bitmap

Drawing Bitmap Graphics on a Canvas

You can draw bitmaps onto a valid Canvas, such as within the onDraw() method of a View, using one of the drawBitmap() methods. For example, the following code loads a Bitmap resource and draws it on a canvas:

```
import android.graphics.Bitmap;

import android.graphics.BitmapFactory;

...

Bitmap pic = BitmapFactory.decodeResource(getResources(),
R.drawable.bluejay);
canvas.drawBitmap(pic, 0, 0, null);
```

Scaling Bitmap Graphics

Perhaps you want to scale your graphic to a smaller size. In this case, you can use the createScaledBitmap() method, like this:

```
Bitmap sm = Bitmap.createScaledBitmap(pic, 50, 75, false);
```
You can preserve the aspect ratio of the Bitmap by checking the getWidth() and getHeight() methods and scaling appropriately.

Shapes

You can define and draw primitive shapes such as rectangles and ovals using the ShapeDrawable class in conjunction with a variety of specialized Shape classes. You can define Paintable drawables as XML resource files, but more often, especially with more complex shapes, this is done programmatically.

Defining Shape Drawables as XML Resources

The following resource file called /res/drawable/green_rect.xml describes a simple, green rectangle shape drawable:

```xml
<?xml version="1.0" encoding="utf-8"?>

<shape xmlns:android="http://schemas.android.com/apk/res/android"
    android:shape="rectangle">
    <solid android:color="#0f0"/>

</shape>
```

You can then load the shape resource and set it as the Drawable as follows:
```
ImageView iView = (ImageView)findViewById(R.id.ImageView1);
iView.setImageResource(R.drawable.green_rect);
```

You should note that many Paint properties can be set via XML as part of the Shape definition. For example, the following Oval shape is defined with a linear gradient (red to white) and stroke style information:

```xml
<?xml version="1.0" encoding="utf-8"?>

<shape xmlns:android="http://schemas.android.com/apk/res/android"
    android:shape="oval">
```

```
<solid android:color="#f00"/>

<gradient android:startColor="#f00"android:endColor="#fff"android:angle="180"
/>

<stroke android:width="3dp" android:color="#00f" android:dashWidth="5dp"
android:dashGap="3dp"
/>

</shape>
```

Defining Shape Drawables Programmatically

You can also define this ShapeDrawable instances programmatically. The different shapes are available as classes within the android.graphics.drawable.shapes package. For example, you can programmatically define the mentioned green rectangle as follows:

```
import android.graphics.drawable.ShapeDrawable; import
android.graphics.drawable.shapes.RectShape;
...
ShapeDrawablerect = new ShapeDrawable(new RectShape());
rect.getPaint().setColor(Color.GREEN);
```

You can then set the Drawable for the ImageView directly:

```
ImageView iView = (ImageView)findViewById(R.id.ImageView1);
iView.setImageDrawable(rect);
```

Drawing Different Shapes

Some of the different shapes available within the android.graphics.drawable.shapes package includes

- Rectangles (and squares)
- Rectangles with rounded corners
- Ovals (and circles)
- Arcs and lines
- Other shapes defined as paths

You can create and use these shapes as Drawable resources directly within ImageView views, or you can find corresponding methods for creating these primitive shapes within a Canvas.

Drawing Rectangles and Squares

Drawing rectangles and squares (rectangles with equal height/width values) is simply a matter of creating a ShapeDrawable from a RectShape object. The RectShape object has no dimensions but is bound by the container object - in this case, the ShapeDrawable.

You can set some basic properties of the ShapeDrawable, such as the Paint color and the default size.

For example, here we create a magenta-colored rectangle that is 100-pixels long and 2-pixels wide, which looks like a straight, horizontal line. We then set the shape as the drawable for an ImageView so the shape can be displayed:

```
import android.graphics.drawable.ShapeDrawable; import
android.graphics.drawable.shapes.RectShape;
...

ShapeDrawablerect = new ShapeDrawable(new RectShape());
rect.setIntrinsicHeight(2);
rect.setIntrinsicWidth(100); rect.getPaint().setColor(Color.MAGENTA);
ImageView iView = (ImageView)findViewById(R.id.ImageView1);
iView.setImageDrawable(rect);
```

Similarly we can draw other shapes.

Frame by Frame Animation

You can think of frame-by-frame animation as a digital flipbook in which a series of similar images display on the screen in a sequence, each subtly different from the last. When you display these images quickly, they give the illusion of movement. This technique is called frame-by-frame animation and is often used on the Web in the form of animated GIF images.

Frame-by-frame animation is best used for complicated graphics transformations that are not easily implemented programmatically.

An object used to create frame-by-frame animations, defined by a series of Drawable objects, which can be used as a View object's background.

The simplest way to create a frame-by-frame animation is to define the animation in an XML file, placed in the res/drawable/ folder, and set it as the background to a View object. Then, call start() to run the animation.

An AnimationDrawable defined in XML consists of a single <animation-list> element and a series of nested <item> tags. Each item defines a frame of the animation. See the example below.

```
spin_animation.xml file in res/drawable/ folder:
<animation-list android:id="@+id/selected" android:oneshot="false">
<item android:drawable="@drawable/wheel0" android:duration="50" />
<item android:drawable="@drawable/wheel1" android:duration="50" />
<item android:drawable="@drawable/wheel2" android:duration="50" />
<item android:drawable="@drawable/wheel3" android:duration="50" />
<item android:drawable="@drawable/wheel4" android:duration="50" />
<item android:drawable="@drawable/wheel5" android:duration="50" />
</animation-list>
```

Here is the code to load and play this animation.

```
// Load the ImageView that will host the animation and

// set its background to our AnimationDrawable XML resource. ImageViewimg =
(ImageView)findViewById(R.id.spinning_wheel_image);
img.setBackgroundResource(R.drawable.spin_animation);
// Get the background, which has been compiled to an AnimationDrawable
object.
AnimationDrawable frameAnimation = (AnimationDrawable)
img.getBackground();
// Start the animation (looped playback by default).
frameAnimation.start();
```

Tweened Animation

With tweened animation, you can provide a single Drawable resource - it is a Bitmap graphic, a ShapeDrawable, a TextView, or any other type of View object and the intermediate frames of the animation are rendered by the system. Android provides tweening support for several common image transformations, including alpha, rotate, scale, and translate animations. You can apply tweened animation transformations to any View, whether it is an ImageView with a Bitmap or shape Drawable, or a layout such as a TableLayout.

Defining Tweening Transformations

You can define tweening transformations as XML resource files or programmatically. All tweened animations share some common properties, including when to start, how long to animate, and whether to return to the starting state upon completion.

Defining Tweened Animations as XML Resources

The following resource file called /res/anim/spin.xml describes a simple five-second rotation:

```
<?xml version="1.0" encoding="utf-8" ?>

<set xmlns:android= "http://schemas.android.com/apk/res/android"
android:shareInterpolator="false">
<rotateandroid:fromDegrees="0" android:toDegrees="360"
```

Defining Tweened Animations Programmatically

You can programmatically define these animations. The different types of transformations are available as classes within the android.view.animation package. For example, you can define the aforementioned rotation animation as follows:

```
import android.view.animation.RotateAnimation;

...

RotateAnimation rotate = new RotateAnimation(0, 360,
RotateAnimation.RELATIVE_TO_SELF, 0.5f,
RotateAnimation.RELATIVE_TO_SELF, 0.5f); rotate.setDuration(5000);
```

Defining Simultaneous and Sequential Tweened Animations

Animation transformations can happen simultaneously or sequentially when you set the startOffset and duration properties, which control when and for how long an animation takes to complete. You can combine animations into the <set> tag (programmatically, using AnimationSet) to share properties.

Loading Animations

Loading animations is made simple by using the AnimationUtils helper class. The following code loads an animation XML resource file called /res/anim/grow.xml and applies it to an ImageView whose source resource is a green rectangle shape drawable:

```
import android.view.animation.Animation;
import android.view.animation.AnimationUtils;

...

ImageView iView = (ImageView)findViewById(R.id.ImageView1);
iView.setImageResource(R.drawable.green_rect);
Animation an =AnimationUtils.loadAnimation(this, R.anim.grow);
iView.startAnimation(an);
```

We can listen for Animation events, including the animation start, end, and repeat events, by implementing an AnimationListener class, such as the MyListener class shown here:

```
class MyListener implements Animation.AnimationListener
{
public void onAnimationEnd(Animation animation)
{
// Do at end of animation
}
public void onAnimationRepeat(Animation animation)
{
// Do each time the animation loops
}
public void onAnimationStart(Animation animation)
{
// Do at start of animation
}}
```

You can then register your AnimationListener as follows:
an.setAnimationListener(new MyListener());

Now let's look at each of the four types of tweening transformations individually. These types are:

- Transparency changes (Alpha)

- Rotations (Rotate)

- Scaling (Scale)

- Movement (Translate)

Working with Alpha Transparency Transformations

Transparency is controlled using Alpha transformations. Alpha transformations can be used to fade objects in and out of view or to layer them on the screen.
Alpha values range from 0.0 (fully transparent or invisible) to 1.0 (fully opaque or visible). Alpha animations involve a starting transparency (fromAlpha) and an ending transparency (toAlpha).

The following XML resource file excerpt defines a transparency - change animation, taking five seconds to fade in from fully transparent to fully opaque:
<alphaandroid:fromAlpha="0.0" android:toAlpha="1.0" android:duration="5000">
</alpha>

Programmatically, you can create this same animation using the AlphaAnimation class within the android.view.animation package.

Working with Rotating Transformations

You can use rotation operations to spin objects clockwise or counter clockwise around a pivot point within the object's boundaries.

Rotations are defined in terms of degrees. For example, you might want an object to make one complete clockwise rotation. To do this, you set the fromDegrees property to 0 and the toDegrees property to 360.To rotate the object counter clockwise instead, you set the toDegrees property to -360. By default, the object pivots around the (0,0) coordinate, or the top-left corner of the object. This is great for rotations such as those of a clock's hands, but much of the time, you want to pivot from the center of the object; you can do this easily by setting the pivot point, which can be a fixed coordinate or a percentage.

The following XML resource file excerpt defines a rotation animation, taking five seconds to make one full clockwise rotation, pivoting from the center of the object:

<rotateandroid:fromDegrees="0" android:toDegrees="360" android:pivotX="50%"
        android:pivotY="50%" android:duration="5000" />

Programmatically, you can create this same animation using the RotateAnimation class within the android.view.animation package.

Working with Scaling Transformations

You can use scaling operations to stretch objects vertically and horizontally. Scaling operations are defined as relative scales. Think of the scale value of 1.0 as 100 percent, or full size. To scale to half-size, or 50 percent, set the target scale value of 0.5. You can scale horizontally and vertically on different scales or on the same scale (to preserve aspect ratio). You need to set four values for proper scaling: starting scale(fromXScale, fromYScale) and target scale (toXScale, toYScale). Again, you can use a pivot point to stretch your object from a specific (x,y) coordinate such as the center or another coordinate.

The following XML resource file excerpt defines a scaling animation, taking five seconds to double an object's size, pivoting from the center of the object:

```
<scaleandroid:pivotX="50%" android:pivotY="50%" android:fromXScale="1.0"
        android:fromYScale="1.0" android:toXScale="2.0" android:toYScale="2.0"
        android:duration="5000" />
```

Programmatically, you can create this same animation using the ScaleAnimation class within the android.view.animation package.

Working with Moving Transformations

You can move objects around using translate operations. Translate operations move an object from one position on the (x,y) coordinate to another coordinate.

To perform a translate operation, you must specify the change, or delta, in the object'scoordinates.You can set four values for translations: starting position (fromXDelta,fromYDelta) and relative target location (toXDelta, toYDelta).

The following XML resource file excerpt defines a translate animation, taking 5 seconds to move an object up (negative) by 100 on the y-axis. We also set the fillAfter property to be true, so the object doesn't "jump" back to its starting position when the animation finishes:

```
<translate    android:toYDelta="-100"

            android:fillAfter="true" android:duration="2500" />
```

Programmatically, you can create this same animation using the TranslateAnimation class within the android.view.animation package.

CHAPTER - 15
Database Connectivity

Connecting to MS SQL

The first thing to do is open a new project in your android studio and create a new empty activity project .

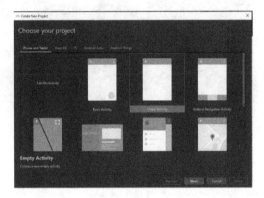

Figure-15a

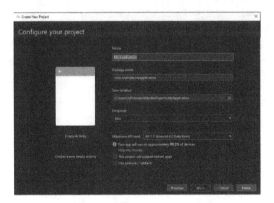

Figure-15b

Once you have created your new project go to the activitymain.xml and add a button then go to its definition by clicking the text tab and add a listener function for click event on the button with the name start.

Figure-15c

Now you have a button its time to give the logic that will connect your application to the data base . go to the mainactivity.java file and write the following code:

```
package in.ajitvoice.dbtestsql;
import android.Manifest;
import android.content.pm.PackageManager;
import android.os.StrictMode;
import android.support.v4.app.ActivityCompat;
import android.support.v7.app.AppCompatActivity;
import android.os.Bundle;
import android.view.View;
import android.widget.Toast;

import java.sql.Connection;
import java.sql.DriverManager;
import java.sql.SQLException;

public class MainActivity extends AppCompatActivity
{
```

6

```java
    private static String ip = "192.168.137.1";
    /* this is the host ip that your data base exists on you can use 10.0.2.2 for local
host
found on your pc. use if config for windows to find the ip if the database exists on
your pc */
    private static String port = "1433";// the port sql server runs on
    private static String Classes = "net.sourceforge.jtds.jdbc.Driver";
    /* the driver that is required for this connection use "org.postgresql.Driver" for
connecting to
postgresql */
    private static String database = "CustomerCareSystem";// the data base name
    private static String username = "ajitdb";// the user name
    private static String password = "1234";// the password
    private static String url = "jdbc:jtds:sqlserver://"+ip+":"+port+"/"+database;
    // the connection url string

private Connection connection = null;
Override
    protected void onCreate(Bundle savedInstanceState) {
        super.onCreate(savedInstanceState);
        setContentView(R.layout.activity_main);
    }

public void start(View view) {
    ActivityCompat.requestPermissions(this, new
String[]{Manifest.permission.INTERNET},
PackageManager.PERMISSION_GRANTED);

    StrictMode.ThreadPolicy policy = new
StrictMode.ThreadPolicy.Builder().permitAll().build();
    StrictMode.setThreadPolicy(policy);
    try {
        Class.forName(Classes);
        connection = DriverManager.getConnection(url, username,password);
        Toast.makeText(this, "Connected", Toast.LENGTH_SHORT).show();
    } catch (ClassNotFoundException e) {
        e.printStackTrace();
        Toast.makeText(this, "Class fail", Toast.LENGTH_SHORT).show();
    } catch (SQLException e) {
```

```
        e.printStackTrace();
        Toast.makeText(this, "Connected no", Toast.LENGTH_SHORT).show();
    }
  }
}
```

Now you have written the above code you need to go to your Gradle scripts and select the build.gradle(Module:app) file and add the following line in the dependencies section.
implementation 'net.sourceforge.jtds:jtds:1.3.1'

Now move on to the Androidmanifest.xml file and add the following lines:

```
<uses-permission android:name="android.permission.INTERNET" />
<uses-permission android:name="android.permission.ACCESS_WIFI_STATE"/>
<uses-permission   android:name="android.permission.ACCESS_NETWORK_STATE"
/>
```

Once you have done all the above steps you can push the play button found on the top right corner and choose your device and your done. When the app starts push the button and a toast will display with the Connected text.

Android SQLite

Android SQLite is a very lightweight database which comes with Android OS. Android SQLite combines a clean SQL interface with a very small memory footprint and decent speed. For Android, SQLite is "baked into" the Android runtime, so every Android application can create its own SQLite databases. Android SQLite native API is not JDBC, as JDBC might be too much overhead for a memory-limited smartphone. Once a database is created successfully its located in data/data//databases/ accessible from Android Device Monitor. SQLite is a typical relational database, containing tables (which consists of rows and columns), indexes etc. We can create our own tables to hold the data accordingly. This structure is referred to as a schema.

SQLite in Android (Android API 31 - SQLite Version 3.32)

So, we know that SQLite is an open-source RDBMS used to perform operations on the databases stored in the form of rows and columns. SQLite is highly supported by Android; in fact, Android comes with the built-in database implementation of SQLite. It is available on each and every Android database and emphasizes scalability, centralization, concurrency, and control. This strives to provide storage at the local level for applications and devices. It is highly economical, efficient, reliable, and independent. It is very simple and doesn't need to be compared with client/server databases.

1. SQLite supports the following three types of data:

- Text Type – to store strings or character type data.
- Integer Type – to store the integer data type.
- Real Type – to store long values.

In SQLite, the data types that are used are termed as valid; it is not validated by SQLite.

2. To use SQLite in Android applications, we use the package android.database.sqlite. This package contains all the APIs to use SQLite.

3. SQLiteOpenHelper is a class that is useful to create the database and manage it.

The two constructors of SQLiteOpenHelper class are:

- SQLiteOpenHelper(Context context, String name, SQLiteDatabase.CursorFactory factory, int version_no) – It creates objects for creating, opening, and managing the database.
- SQLiteOpenHelper(Context context, String name, SQLiteDatabase.CursorFactory factory, int version_no, DatabaseErrorHandler errorHandler) – Its object specifies the error handler along with creating, opening, and managing the database.

4. SQLiteDatabase is a class that has methods to perform operations such as create, update, delete, etc.

Features of Android SQLite

SQLite has many features which it supports as follows:

- Full-featured SQL implementation along with various advanced capabilities such as partial indexing, JSON, and some other.
- Very simple with easy to use API.
- Has a really fast execution at times, and it is even faster than the direct file system Input-Output.
- Self-dependent as it has no external dependencies.
- Transactions in SQlite also have the ACID property that is – Atomicity, Consistency, Isolation, and Durability.
- Cross-platform as it supports Android, iOS, Linux, Mac, Windows, VxWorks, Solaris. It is easy to port it to other systems.
- Comes along with a standalone command-line interface client.
- Completely stored in a single cross-platform.
- Written completely in ANSI-C.
- Highly lightweight and small, as it is possible to configure it in less than 400Kbs. If configured by omitting the optional features, it uses less than 250Kbs.

How To Download & Install SQLite Tools

you will learn step by step on how to download and use the SQLite tools to your computer.

Download SQLite tools

To download SQLite, you open the download page of the SQlite official website.

First, go to the https://www.sqlite.org website.

Second, open the download page https://www.sqlite.org/download.html

SQLite provides various tools for working across platforms e.g., Windows, Linux, and Mac. You need to select an appropriate version to download.

For example, to work with SQLite on Windows, you download the command-line shell program as shown in the screenshot below.

Precompiled Binaries for Windows

sqlite-dll-win32-x86-3290000.zip (474.63 KiB)	32-bit DLL (x86) for SQLite version 3.29.0. (sha1: 00435a36f5e6059287cde2cebb2882669cdba3a5)
sqlite-dll-win64-x64-3290000.zip (788.61 KiB)	64-bit DLL (x64) for SQLite version 3.29.0. (sha1: c88204328d6ee3ff49ca0d58cbbee05243172c3a)
sqlite-tools-win32-x86-3290000.zip (1.71 MiB)	A bundle of command-line tools for managing SQLite database files, including the command-line shell program, the sqldiff.exe program, and the sqlite3_analyzer.exe program. (sha1: f009ff42b8c22886675005e3e57c94d62bca12b3)

Figure-15d

The downloaded file is in the ZIP format and its size is quite small.

Run SQLite tools

Installing SQLite is simple and straightforward.

First, create a new folder e.g., C:\sqlite.

Second, extract the content of the file that you downloaded in the previous section to the C:\sqlite folder. You should see three programs in the C:\sqlite folder as shown below:

sqldiff.exe
sqlite3.exe
sqlite3_analyzer.exe

Figure-15e

11

First, open the command line window:

Figure-15f

and navigate to the C:\sqlite folder.

C:\cd c:\sqlite

C:\sqlite>

Second, type sqlite3 and press enter, you should see the following output:

C:\sqlite>sqlite3

SQLite version 3.29.0 2019-07-10 17:32:03

Enter ".help" for usage hints.

Connected to a transient in-memory database.

Use ".open FILENAME" to reopen on a persistent database.

sqlite>

Third, you can type the .help command from the sqlite> prompt to see all available commands in sqlite3.

sqlite> .help

.archive ...   Manage SQL archives: ".archive --help" for details

.auth ON|OFF   Show authorizer callbacks

.backup ?DB? FILE   Backup DB (default "main") to FILE

.bail on|off   Stop after hitting an error. Default OFF

.binary on|off   Turn binary output on or off. Default OFF

.cd DIRECTORY   Change the working directory to DIRECTORY

...

Fourth, to quit the sqlite>, you use .quit command as follows:

sqlite> .quit

c:\sqlite>

Install SQLite GUI tool

The sqlite3 shell is excellent...

However, sometimes, you may want to work with the SQLite databases using an intuitive GUI tool.

There are many GUI tools for managing SQLite databases available ranging from freeware to commercial licenses.

SQLiteStudio

The SQLiteStudio tool is a free GUI tool for managing SQLite databases. It is free, portable, intuitive, and cross-platform. SQLite tool also provides some of the most important features to work with SQLite databases such as importing, exporting data in various formats including CSV, XML, and JSON.

You can download the SQLiteStudio installer or its portable version by visiting the download page. Then, you can extract (or install) the download file to a folder e.g., C:\sqlite\gui\ and launch it.

The following picture illustrates how to launch the SQLiteStudio:

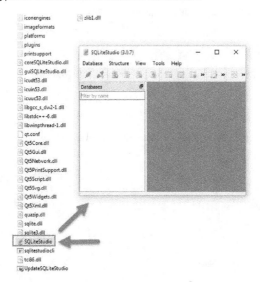

Figure-15g

Other SQLite GUI tools

Besides the SQLite Studio, you can use the following free SQLite GUI tools:

DBeaver is another free multi-platform database tool. It supports all popular major relational database systems MySQL, PostgreSQL, Oracle, DB2, SQL Server, Sybase.. including SQLite.

DB Browser for SQLite – is an open-source tool to manage database files compatible with SQLite.

Now, you should be ready to work with SQLite.

Trying SQLite on an Android Virtual Device (AVD)

For readers unfamiliar with databases in general and SQLite in particular, diving right into creating an Android application that uses SQLite may seem a little intimidating. Fortunately, Android is shipped with SQLite pre-installed, including an interactive environment for issuing SQL commands from within an adb shell session connected to a running Android AVD emulator instance. This is both a useful way to learn about SQLite and SQL, and also an invaluable tool for identifying problems with databases created by applications running in an emulator.

To launch an interactive SQLite session, begin by running an AVD session. This can be achieved from within Android Studio by launching the Android Virtual Device Manager (Tools -> Android -> AVD Manager), selecting a previously configured AVD and clicking on Start.

Once the AVD is up and running, open a Terminal or Command-Prompt window and connect to the emulator using the adb command-line tool as follows (note that the −e flag directs the tool to look for an emulator with which to connect, rather than a physical device):

adb −e shell

Once connected, the shell environment will provide a command prompt at which commands may be entered:

root@android:/ #

Data stored in SQLite databases are actually stored in database files on the file system of the Android device on which the application is running. By default, the file system path for these database files is as follows:

/data/data/<package name>/databases/<database filename>.db

For example, if an application with the package name com.example.MyDBApp creates a database named mydatabase.db, the path to the file on the device would read as follows:

/data/data/com.example.MyDBApp/databases/mydatabase.db

For the purposes of this exercise, therefore, change directory to /data/data within the adb shell and create a sub-directory hierarchy suitable for some SQLite experimentation:

cd /data/data

mkdir com.example.dbexample

cd com.example.dbexample

```
mkdir databases

cd databases
```

With a suitable location created for the database file, launch the interactive SQLite tool as follows:

root@android:/data/data/databases # sqlite3 ./mydatabase.db

sqlite3 ./mydatabase.db

SQLite version 3.7.4

Enter ".help" for instructions

Enter SQL statements terminated with a ";"

sqlite>

At the sqlite> prompt, commands may be entered to perform tasks such as creating tables and inserting and retrieving data. For example, to create a new table in our database with fields to hold ID, name, address and phone number fields the following statement is required:

sqlite> create table contacts (_id integer primary key autoincrement, name text, address text, phone text);

Android SQLite SQLiteOpenHelper

Android has features available to handle changing database schemas, which mostly depend on using the SQLiteOpenHelper class. SQLiteOpenHelper is designed to get rid of two very common problems.

- When the application runs the first time At this point, we do not yet have a database. So we will have to create the tables, indexes, starter data, and so on.
- When the application is upgraded to a newer schema Our database will still be on the old schema from the older edition of the app. We will have option to alter the database schema to match the needs of the rest of the app.

SQLiteOpenHelper wraps up these logic to create and upgrade a database as per our specifications. For that we'll need to create a custom subclass of SQLiteOpenHelper implementing at least the following three methods.

Constructor : This takes the Context (e.g., an Activity), the name of the database, an optional cursor factory (we'll discuss this later), and an integer representing the version of the database schema you are using (typically starting from 1 and increment later).

```
public DatabaseHelper(Context context)
{
super(context, DB_NAME, null, DB_VERSION);
}
```

- onCreate (SQLiteDatabase db) It's called when there is no database and the app needs one. It passes us a SQLiteDatabase object, pointing to a newly-created database, that we can populate with tables and initial data.

- onUpgrade (SQLiteDatabase db, int oldVersion, int newVersion) It's called when the schema version we need does not match the schema version of the database, It passes us a SQLiteDatabase object and the old and new version numbers.

Hence we can figure out the best way to convert the database from the old schema to the new one.

In Android, the SQLiteDatabase namespace defines the functionality to connect and manage a database. It provides functionality to create, delete, manage and display database content.

Create a Database

Simple steps to create a database and handle are as following.

1. Create "SQLiteDatabase" object.
2. Open or Create database and create connection.
3. Perform insert, update or delete operation.
4. Cursor to display data from table of database.
5. Close the database connectivity.

Step 1: Instantiate "SQLiteDatabase" object

SQLiteDatabase db;
Before you can use the above object, you must import the android.database.sqlite.SQLiteDatabasenamespace in your application.
db=openOrCreateDatabase(String path, int mode, SQLiteDatabase.CursorFactory factory)

This method is used to create/open database. As the name suggests, it will open a database connection if it is already there, otherwise it will create a new one.
Example,
db=openOrCreateDatabase("XYZ_Database",SQLiteDatabase.CREATE_IF_NECESSARY,null);

Arguments:
String path - Name of the database
Int mode - operating mode. Use 0 or "MODE_PRIVATE" for the default operation, or "CREATE_IF_NECESSARY" if you like to give option that "if database is not there, create it"
CursorFactory factory - An optional factory class that is called to instantiate a cursor when query is called

Step 2: Execute DDL command

db.execSQL(String sql) throws SQLException

This command is used to execute single SQL statement which doesn't return any data means other than SELECT or any other.
In the above example, it takes "CREATE TABLE" statement of SQL. This will create a table of "Integer" & "Text" fields.
Try and Catch block is require while performing this operation. An exception that indicates there was an error with SQL parsing or execution.

Step 3: Create object of "ContentValues" and Initiate it.

ContentValues values=new ContentValues();
This class is used to store a set of values. We can also say, it will map ColumnName and relavent ColumnValue.
values.put("id", eid.getText().toString());
values.put("name", ename.getText().toString());

String Key - Name of field as in table. Ex. "id", "name"
String Value - Value to be inserted.

Step 4: Perform Insert Statement.

insert(String table, String nullColumnHack, ContentValues values)

String table - Name of table related to database.
String nullColumnHack - If not set to null, the nullColumnHack parameter provides the name of nullable column name to explicitly insert a NULL into in the case where yourvalues is empty.

ContentValues values - This map contains the initial column values for the row.
This method returns a long. The row ID of the newly inserted row, or -1 if an error occurred.
Example,
db.insert("temp", null, values);

Step 5: Create Cursor

This interface provides random read-write access to the result set returned by a database query.
Cursor c=db.rawQuery(String sql, String[] selectionArgs)

Strign sql - The SQL query

String []selectionArgs - You may include ?s in where clause in the query, which will be replaced by the values from selectionArgs. The values will be bound as Strings.

Example,
Cursor c=db.rawQuery("SELECT * FROM temp",null);
If not set to null, the nullColumnHack parameter provides the name of nullable column name to explicitly insert a NULL into in the case where yourvalues is empty.

Methods
moveToFirst Moves cursor pointer at first position of result set
moveToNext Moves cursor pointer next to current position.
isAfterLast Returs false, if cursor pointer is not at last position of result set.

Step 6: Close Cursor and Close Database connectivity
Example,
c.moveToFirst();
while(!c.isAfterLast())
{
//statements
c.moveToNext();
}

CRUD Operations

We define a DBManager class to perform all database CRUD Create, Read, Update and Delete) operations.

Opening and Closing Android SQLite Database Connection

Before performing any database operations like insert, update, delete records in a table, first open the database connection by calling getWritableDatabase() method as shown below:

```
public DBManager open() throws SQLException
{
dbHelper = new DatabaseHelper(context); database =
dbHelper.getWritableDatabase(); return this;
}
```

The dbHelper is an instance of the subclass of SQLiteOpenHelper . To close a database connection the following method is invoked.

```
public void close()
{
dbHelper.close();
}
```

Inserting new Record into Android SQLite database table

The following code snippet shows how to insert a new record in the android SQLite database.

```
public void insert(String name, String desc)
{
ContentValues contentValue = new ContentValues();
contentValue.put(DatabaseHelper.SUBJECT, name);
contentValue.put(DatabaseHelper.DESC, desc);
database.insert(DatabaseHelper.TABLE_NAME, null, contentValue);
}
```

Content Values creates an empty set of values using the given initial size. We'll discuss the other instance values when we jump into the coding part.

Updating Record in Android SQLite database table

The following snippet shows how to update a single record.

```
public int update(long _id, String name, String desc)
{
ContentValues contentValues = new ContentValues();
contentValues.put(DatabaseHelper.SUBJECT, name);
contentValues.put(DatabaseHelper.DESC, desc);
int    i    =    database.update(DatabaseHelper.TABLE_NAME,    contentValues,
DatabaseHelper._ID + " = " + _id, null);
return i;
}
```

Deleting a Record

We just need to pass the id of the record to be deleted as shown below.
```
public void delete(long _id)
{
database.delete(DatabaseHelper.TABLE_NAME, DatabaseHelper._ID + "=" + _id,
null);
}
```

Android SQLite Cursor

A Cursor represents the entire result set of the query. Once the query is fetched a call to cursor.moveToFirst() is made. Calling moveToFirst() does two things:
It allows us to test whether the query returned an empty set (by testing the return value)
It moves the cursor to the first result (when the set is not empty) The following code is used to fetch all records:
```
public Cursor fetch()
{
    String[ ] columns = new String[ ]
    {
    DatabaseHelper._ID, DatabaseHelper.SUBJECT, DatabaseHelper.DESC };
```

```
    Cursor cursor = database.query(DatabaseHelper.TABLE_NAME, columns, null,
null, null, null, null);
    if (cursor != null)
    {
      cursor.moveToFirst();
    }
    return cursor;
  }
```

Another way to use a Cursor is to wrap it in a CursorAdapter . Just as ArrayAdapter
adapts arrays, CursorAdapter adapts Cursor objects, making their data available to
an AdapterView like a ListView.

Android SQLite Application

In this application we wish to create records that store Country names and their respective currencies in the form of a ListView. We cover all the features discusses above.

The application consists of 5 classes. We begin with defining with DatabaseHelper, which is a subclass of SQLiteOpenHelper as follows: DatabaseHelper.java

```java
package in.ajitvoice.sqlite;
import android.content.Context;
import android.database.sqlite.SQLiteDatabase;
import android.database.sqlite.SQLiteOpenHelper;
public class DatabaseHelper extends SQLiteOpenHelper
{
// Table Name
public static final String TABLE_NAME = "COUNTRIES";

// Table columns
public static final String _ID = "_id";
public static final String SUBJECT = "subject"; public static final String DESC =
"description";

// Database Information
static final String DB_NAME = "AJITVOICE_COUNTRIES.DB";

// database version
static final int DB_VERSION = 1;

// Creating table query
private static final String CREATE_TABLE = "create table " + TABLE_NAME +
+ " INTEGER PRIMARY KEY AUTOINCREMENT, " + SUBJECT + " TEXT NOT NULL, " +
DESC + " TEXT);";

public DatabaseHelper(Context context)
{
super(context, DB_NAME, null, DB_VERSION);
}
```

```java
@Override
public void onCreate(SQLiteDatabase db)
{
db.execSQL(CREATE_TABLE);
}

@Override
public void onUpgrade(SQLiteDatabase db, int oldVersion, int newVersion)
{
db.execSQL("DROP TABLE IF EXISTS " + TABLE_NAME);
onCreate(db);
}}
```

As discussed above we have overridden the onCreate() and onUpgrade() methods besides the constructor. We've assigned the names to the database and the table as AJITVOICE_COUNTRIES.DB and COUNTRIES respectively. The index column is auto incremented whenever a new row is inserted. The column names for country and currency are "subject" and "description". The DBManager classes is where the DatabaseHelper is initialized and the CRUD Operations are defined. Below is the code for this class: DBManager.java

```java
package in.ajitvoice.sqlite;
import android.content.ContentValues;
import android.content.Context;
import android.database.Cursor;
import android.database.SQLException;
import android.database.sqlite.SQLiteDatabase;
public class DBManager
{
private DatabaseHelper dbHelper;
private Context context;
private SQLiteDatabase database;
public DBManager(Context c)
{
context = c;
}
```

```
public DBManager open() throws SQLException
{
dbHelper = new DatabaseHelper(context);
database = dbHelper.getWritableDatabase();
return this;
}

public void close()
{
dbHelper.close();
}

public void insert(String name, String desc)
{
ContentValues contentValue = new ContentValues();
contentValue.put(DatabaseHelper.SUBJECT, name);
contentValue.put(DatabaseHelper.DESC, desc);
database.insert(DatabaseHelper.TABLE_NAME, null, contentValue);
}

public Cursor fetch()
{
String[ ] columns = new String[ ] { DatabaseHelper._ID, DatabaseHelper.SUBJECT,
DatabaseHelper.DESC };}
Cursor cursor = database.query(DatabaseHelper.TABLE_NAME, columns, null, null,
null, null, null);
    if (cursor != null)
    {
        cursor.moveToFirst();
    }
    return cursor;
}

public int update(long _id, String name, String desc)
{
ContentValues contentValues = new ContentValues();
contentValues.put(DatabaseHelper.SUBJECT, name);
contentValues.put(DatabaseHelper.DESC, desc);
```

```
int i = database.update(DatabaseHelper.TABLE_NAME, contentValues,
DatabaseHelper._ID + " = " + _id, null);
  return i;
}

public void delete(long _id)
{
database.delete(DatabaseHelper.TABLE_NAME, DatabaseHelper._ID + "=" +
}
}
```

The CountryListActivity.java class is the activity which is launched when the application starts. Below is layout defined for it: fragment_emp_list.xml

```xml
<?xml version="1.0" encoding="utf-8"?>
<RelativeLayout xmlns:android="https://schemas.android.com/apk/res/android"
android:layout_width="fill_parent"
android:layout_height="fill_parent" >

<ListView
android:id="@+id/list_view" android:layout_width="match_parent"
android:layout_height="wrap_content" android:dividerHeight="1dp"
android:padding="10dp" >
</ListView>

<TextView
android:id="@+id/empty" android:layout_width="wrap_content"
android:layout_height="wrap_content" android:layout_centerInParent="true"
android:text="@string/empty_list_text" />
</RelativeLayout>
```

Here a ListView component is defined to included the records stored in the database. Initially the ListView would be empty hence a TextView is used to display the same.

CountryListActivity.java

```java
package in.ajitvoice.sqlite;
import android.content.Intent; import android.database.Cursor; import
android.os.Bundle;
import android.support.v4.widget.SimpleCursorAdapter;
import android.support.v7.app.ActionBarActivity; import android.view.Menu;
import android.view.MenuItem; import android.view.View;
import android.widget.AdapterView;
import android.widget.ListView; import android.widget.TextView;

public class CountryListActivity extends ActionBarActivity
{
private DBManager dbManager;
private ListView listView;

private SimpleCursorAdapter adapter;
final String[ ] from = new String[ ] { DatabaseHelper._ID, DatabaseHelper.SUBJECT,
DatabaseHelper.DESC };
final int[ ] to = new int[ ] { R.id.id, R.id.title, R.id.desc };

@Override
protected void onCreate(Bundle savedInstanceState)
{
super.onCreate(savedInstanceState);
setContentView(R.layout.fragment_emp_list);
dbManager = new DBManager(this);
dbManager.open();
Cursor cursor = dbManager.fetch();
listView = (ListView) findViewById(R.id.list_view);
listView.setEmptyView(findViewById(R.id.empty));
adapter = new SimpleCursorAdapter(this, R.layout.activity_view_record, cursor, from,
to, 0);
adapter.notifyDataSetChanged();

listView.setAdapter(adapter);
// OnCLickListiner For List Items
    listView.setOnItemClickListener(new AdapterView.OnItemClickListener() {
      @Override
```

```java
        public void onItemClick(AdapterView<?> parent, View view, int position, long
viewId) {
            TextView idTextView = (TextView) view.findViewById(R.id.id);
            TextView titleTextView = (TextView) view.findViewById(R.id.title);
            TextView descTextView = (TextView) view.findViewById(R.id.desc);

            String id = idTextView.getText().toString();
            String title = titleTextView.getText().toString();
            String desc = descTextView.getText().toString();

            Intent modify_intent = new Intent(getApplicationContext(),
ModifyCountryActivity.class);
            modify_intent.putExtra("title", title);
            modify_intent.putExtra("desc", desc);
            modify_intent.putExtra("id", id);

            startActivity(modify_intent);
        }
    });
}

@Override
public boolean onCreateOptionsMenu(Menu menu) {
    getMenuInflater().inflate(R.menu.main, menu);
    return true;
}

@Override
public boolean onOptionsItemSelected(MenuItem item)
{
    int id = item.getItemId();
    if (id == R.id.add_record)
    {
        Intent add_mem = new Intent(this, AddCountryActivity.class);
        startActivity(add_mem);
    }
    return super.onOptionsItemSelected(item);
}
}
```

In this activity the DBManager object is invoked to perform the CRUD Operations. A SimpleCursorAdapter is defined to add elements to the list from the query results that are returned in an Cursor Object. On list item click an intent is performed to open the ModifyCountryActivity class. The menu contains an item to add a new record from the ActionBar. Here again an intent is performed to open the AddCountryActivity class.

Below is menu.xml code. menu.xml

```xml
<menu xmlns:android="https://schemas.android.com/apk/res/android"
xmlns:app="https://schemas.android.com/apk/res-auto"
xmlns:tools="https://schemas.android.com/tools"
tools:context="in.ajitvoice.sqlitesample.MainActivity" >

<item
android:id="@+id/add_record" android:icon="@android:drawable/ic_menu_add"
android:orderInCategory="100" android:title="@string/add_record"
app:showAsAction="always"/>

</menu>
```

The xml layout and code of AddCountryActivity.java file are defined below:
activity_add_record.xml

```xml
<?xml version="1.0" encoding="utf-8"?>
<LinearLayout xmlns:android="https://schemas.android.com/apk/res/android"
android:layout_width="match_parent" android:layout_height="match_parent"
android:orientation="vertical" android:padding="20dp" >

<EditText
android:id="@+id/subject_edittext" android:layout_width="match_parent"
android:layout_height="wrap_content" android:ems="10"
android:hint="@string/enter_title" >
<requestFocus />
</EditText>
```

```
<EditText
android:id="@+id/description_edittext" android:layout_width="match_parent"
android:layout_height="wrap_content" android:ems="10"
android:hint="@string/enter_desc" android:inputType="textMultiLine"
android:minLines="5" >
</EditText>

<Button
android:id="@+id/add_record" android:layout_width="wrap_content"
android:layout_height="wrap_content" android:layout_gravity="center"
android:text="@string/add_record" />

</LinearLayout>
```

Two EditText components that take the inputs for country and currency along with a
button to add the values to the database and display it in the ListView are defined.

AddCountryActivity.java

```
package in.ajitvoice.sqlite;
import android.app.Activity;
import android.content.Intent;
import android.os.Bundle;
import android.view.View;
import android.view.View.OnClickListener;
import android.widget.Button;
import android.widget.EditText;
public class AddCountryActivity extends Activity implements OnClickListener
{
private Button addTodoBtn;
private EditText subjectEditText; private EditText descEditText;

private DBManager dbManager;

@Override
protected void onCreate(Bundle savedInstanceState)
{
super.onCreate(savedInstanceState);
```

```java
setTitle("Add Record"); setContentView(R.layout.activity_add_record);
subjectEditText = (EditText) findViewById(R.id.subject_edittext);
descEditText = (EditText) findViewById(R.id.description_edittext);
addTodoBtn = (Button) findViewById(R.id.add_record);
dbManager = new DBManager(this);
dbManager.open();
addTodoBtn.setOnClickListener(this);
}

@Override
public void onClick(View v)
{
switch (v.getId())
{
case R.id.add_record:

final String name = subjectEditText.getText().toString();
final String desc = descEditText.getText().toString();

dbManager.insert(name, desc);

Intent main = new Intent(AddCountryActivity.this, CountryListA
.setFlags(Intent.FLAG_ACTIVITY_CLEAR_TOP);

startActivity(main);
break;
}
}
}
```

The CRUD operation performed here is adding a new record to the database. The xml layout and code of ModifyCountryActivity.java file are defined below:
activity_modify_record.xml

```xml
<?xml version="1.0" encoding="utf-8"?>
<LinearLayout xmlns:android="https://schemas.android.com/apk/res/android"
android:layout_width="match_parent" android:layout_height="match_parent"
android:orientation="vertical" android:padding="10dp" >
```

```xml
<EditText
android:id="@+id/subject_edittext" android:layout_width="match_parent"
android:layout_height="wrap_content" android:layout_marginBottom="10dp"
android:ems="10" android:hint="@string/enter_title" />

<EditText
android:id="@+id/description_edittext" android:layout_width="match_parent"
android:layout_height="wrap_content" android:ems="10"
android:hint="@string/enter_desc" android:inputType="textMultiLine"
android:minLines="5" >
</EditText>

<LinearLayout
android:layout_width="fill_parent" android:layout_height="wrap_content"
android:weightSum="2" android:gravity="center_horizontal"
android:orientation="horizontal" >

<Button
android:id="@+id/btn_update" android:layout_width="wrap_content"
android:layout_height="wrap_content" android:layout_weight="1"
android:text="@string/btn_update" />

<Button
android:id="@+id/btn_delete" android:layout_width="wrap_content"
android:layout_height="wrap_content" android:layout_weight="1"
android:text="@string/btn_delete" />
</LinearLayout>
</LinearLayout>
```

It's similar to the previous layout except that modify and delete buttons are added.

ModifyCountryActivity.java

```java
package in.ajitvoice.sqlite;
import android.app.Activity;
import android.content.Intent;
import android.os.Bundle;
import android.view.View;
import android.view.View.OnClickListener;
import android.widget.Button;
import android.widget.EditText;
public class ModifyCountryActivity extends Activity implements OnClickListener
private EditText titleText;
private Button updateBtn, deleteBtn;
private EditText descText;
private long _id;
private DBManager dbManager; @Override
protected void onCreate(Bundle savedInstanceState)
{
super.onCreate(savedInstanceState);
setTitle("Modify Record"); setContentView(R.layout.activity_modify_record);
dbManager = new DBManager(this); dbManager.open();

titleText = (EditText) findViewById(R.id.subject_edittext);
descText = (EditText) findViewById(R.id.description_edittext);

updateBtn = (Button) findViewById(R.id.btn_update);
deleteBtn = (Button) findViewById(R.id.btn_delete);

Intent intent = getIntent();
String id = intent.getStringExtra("id");
String name = intent.getStringExtra("title");
String desc = intent.getStringExtra("desc");
_id = Long.parseLong(id); titleText.setText(name);
```

```
descText.setText(desc);
updateBtn.setOnClickListener(this);
deleteBtn.setOnClickListener(this);
}
@Override
public void onClick(View v)
{
switch (v.getId())
{
case R.id.btn_update:
String title = titleText.getText().toString();
String desc = descText.getText().toString();
dbManager.update(_id, title, desc);
this.returnHome();
break;

case R.id.btn_delete:
dbManager.delete(_id);
this.returnHome();
break;
}
}

public void returnHome()
{
Intent home_intent = new Intent(getApplicationContext(), CountryListAc
.setFlags(Intent.FLAG_ACTIVITY_CLEAR_TOP);
startActivity(home_intent);
}
}
```

The CRUD operations performed here are updating and deleting a record. The below images are the screenshots of the final output of our project. The first image is the output seen when the application is launched for the first time.

Figure-15h

The second image is the result of clicking the menu option from the ActionBar to add a new record as shown below. The third image shows an output when 3 records are added :

Figure-15i

The fourth image shows the output when any list item is clicked to modify or delete a record :

Figure-15j

The final image is the output when a record is deleted. In this example we delete the first record :

Figure-15k

Connect Android to MySQL Database using mysql-connector.jar.

You can download Jar Library using this Link
http://www.java2s.com/Code/Jar/m/Downloadmysqlconnectorjar.htm

Android Connect MySQL Database Programmatically :

Create a new Android Application in Android Studio with

Package name : in.ajitvoice.mysqlapp

Application name : MySQLApp

You can always name your Package and Application name according to your requirements.

Application Working :

Application will first try to connect with the MySQL Database and on successful Database connection, android application will display data from a table on a Android TextView. It will connect via IP address of the Database with a correct Database Credentials.

MySQL Database Script :

create schema myDB

use myDB

create table tblCountries
(
ID int NOT NULL AUTO_INCREMENT primary key,
Country varchar(255) NOT NULL
)

Insert into tblCountries (Country) values ('India')
Insert into tblCountries (Country) values ('Australia')
Insert into tblCountries (Country) values ('Mauritius')
Insert into tblCountries (Country) values ('USA')
Insert into tblCountries (Country) values ('England')
Insert into tblCountries (Country) values ('New Zealand')
Insert into tblCountries (Country) values ('Spain')

Select * from tblCountries
select distinct Country from tblCountries
Now, open your activity_main.xml file and edit it as below :

activity_main.xml:

```xml
<?xml version="1.0" encoding="utf-8"?>
<LinearLayout xmlns:android="http://schemas.android.com/apk/res/android"
xmlns:app="http://schemas.android.com/apk/res-auto"
xmlns:tools="http://schemas.android.com/tools"
android:layout_width="match_parent"
android:layout_height="match_parent"
android:fitsSystemWindows="true"
android:orientation="vertical"
android:padding="5dp">

<TextView
android:layout_width="match_parent"
android:layout_height="wrap_content"
android:layout_margin="5dp"
android:padding="5dp"
android:text="Android MySQL Application"
android:textColor="@color/colorAccent"
android:textSize="20sp"
android:textStyle="bold" />

<TextView
android:id="@+id/txtData"
android:layout_width="match_parent"
android:layout_height="wrap_content"
android:layout_margin="2dp"
android:text="Your Data will be Displayed here"
android:textStyle="bold" />

<Button
android:id="@+id/btnFetch"
android:layout_width="wrap_content"
android:layout_height="wrap_content"
android:layout_gravity="center_horizontal"
android:layout_margin="2dp"
android:background="@color/colorPrimaryDark"
android:minWidth="250dp"
android:text="Fetch Data"
android:textColor="#fff" />

<Button
android:id="@+id/btnClear"
android:layout_width="wrap_content"
android:layout_height="wrap_content"
android:layout_gravity="center_horizontal"
android:layout_margin="2dp"
android:background="@color/colorAccent"
android:minWidth="250dp"
android:text="Clear"
android:textColor="#fff" />
```

</LinearLayout>

The layout contains a Android TextView to show our Table data from MySQL Database and two buttons, one for connecting to Database and other for clearing the TextView content.

Figure-15l

Now, let's code it.

MainActivity.java:

```java
package in.ajitvoice.mysqlapp;

import android.os.AsyncTask;
import android.os.Bundle;
import android.support.v7.app.AppCompatActivity;
import android.view.View;
import android.widget.Button;
import android.widget.TextView;
import android.widget.Toast;

import java.sql.Connection;
import java.sql.DriverManager;
import java.sql.ResultSet;
import java.sql.ResultSetMetaData;
import java.sql.Statement;

public class MainActivity extends AppCompatActivity {

private static final String url = "jdbc:mysql://192.168.0.192:3306/myDB";
private static final String user = "ajit";
private static final String pass = "1234";
Button btnFetch,btnClear;
TextView txtData;

@Override
protected void onCreate(Bundle savedInstanceState) {
```

```java
super.onCreate(savedInstanceState);
setContentView(R.layout.activity_main);
txtData = (TextView) this.findViewById(R.id.txtData);
btnFetch = (Button) findViewById(R.id.btnFetch);
btnClear = (Button) findViewById(R.id.btnClear);
btnFetch.setOnClickListener(new View.OnClickListener() {

@Override
public void onClick(View v) {
// TODO Auto-generated method stub
ConnectMySql connectMySql = new ConnectMySql();
connectMySql.execute("");
}
});
btnClear.setOnClickListener(new View.OnClickListener() {
@Override
public void onClick(View view) {
txtData.setText("");
}
});
}

private class ConnectMySql extends AsyncTask<String, Void, String> {
String res = "";

@Override
protected void onPreExecute() {
super.onPreExecute();
Toast.makeText(MainActivity.this, "Please wait...", Toast.LENGTH_SHORT)
.show();

}

@Override
protected String doInBackground(String... params) {
try {
Class.forName("com.mysql.jdbc.Driver");
Connection con = DriverManager.getConnection(url, user, pass);
System.out.println("Databaseection success");

String result = "Database Connection Successful\n";
Statement st = con.createStatement();
ResultSet rs = st.executeQuery("select distinct Country from tblCountries");
ResultSetMetaData rsmd = rs.getMetaData();

while (rs.next()) {
result += rs.getString(1).toString() + "\n";
}
res = result;
} catch (Exception e) {
e.printStackTrace();
res = e.toString();
}
```

```
return res;
}

@Override
protected void onPostExecute(String result) {
txtData.setText(result);
}}}
```

And now run your application. On Pressing on the "Fetch Data" button it will fetch Data from MySQL Database table.

Figure-15m

How to view the data stored in sqlite in android studio?

Follow the following steps to view the database and its data stored in android sqlite:

Figure-15n

- Open File Explorer.
- Go to data directory inside data directory.
- Search for your application package name.
- Inside your application package go to databases where you will found your database (contactsManager).
- Save your database (contactsManager) anywhere you like.
- Download any SqLite browser plugins or tool (in my case DB Browser for SQLite).
- Launch DB Browser for SQLite and open your database (contactsManager).
- Go to Browse Data -> select your table (contacts) you will see the data stored

CHAPTER - 16
Generate & Publish Applications

Android Studio allows you to create two kinds of APK files.

First are the debug APK files that are generated solely for testing purposes. They will run on your Android mobile. However, they cannot be uploaded to the Play Store or made available to the public.

Secondly, you can generate signed APK files. Signed APK files come in handy when you've tested your application and it is ready to be uploaded on the Play Store and released to the general public.

First things first: open up a project file in Android Studio. If you don't have a project file yet, simply create a New Project.

Creating an APK file
Generating a debug APK file is easy and is a matter of just a few clicks.

First, open up your project or application that you want to import into an APK file. Then, select Build > Build Bundle(s)/APK(s) > Build APK(s) from the toolbar menu.

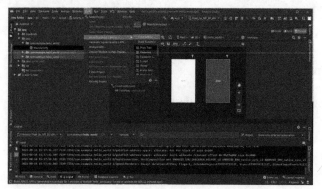

Figure-16a

Android Studio will take a few moments to generate an APK file.

Once the APK build is complete, you'll receive a notification on the bottom right corner of your screen. From that notification, select Locate and you will be led to the APK file location.

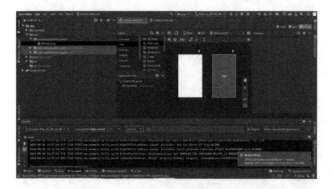

Figure-16b

If you miss the notification, you can still locate the APK file in the following path within your project folder: app/build/outputs/apk/debug. The file is named app-debug.apk by default.

Creating a Signed APK File

To generate a signed APK file, open the Build menu from the toolbar and select Generate Signed Bundle/APK.

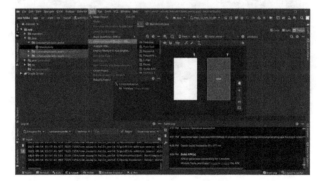

Figure-16c

This opens up a screen where you have to select between creating an Android App Bundle and creating an APK file. Check the APK radio button and proceed to the next window.

45

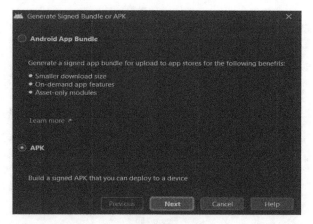

Figure-16d

In the next window, you will be shown the module (your application) for which the APK file is being generated. You'll be asked about your Key store path, Key store password, Key alias, and the Key password.

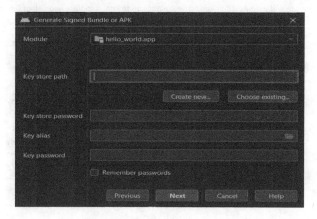

Figure-16e

Creating a New Key Store

Assuming that this is the first time you're creating a Signed APK file, you will have to create a new key store.

Keys are used by the developer to access their application once it has been uploaded to the Play Store. The need for the keys usually arises when you have to update your application. All of the keys are stored in the key store.

Both the key store and the keys are protected by passwords of their own. The passwords should be at least six characters in length. Also, it is a good practice to keep multiple copies of your keys since they are your only gateway to your application. If the key is lost, you will not be able to access your application or update it. Creating your own app requires you to create a new key store. To do so, select Create new. You will find it underneath the input field where you enter the key store path.

Figure-16f

You will then be redirected to a new window.

Figure-16g

In the new window, enter the path for your new key store, and then enter a password to protect it.

In the same window, you will also be setting a new key for your application. Enter an identity for your key in the key alias field and then enter a password for it.

You can keep the same password as that of your key store, but it's a good practice to give a new password to each of your keys. The same goes for the key alias.

The next field defines the validity of your application. This is the duration after which the key to your application will expire, leaving your application inaccessible. The default validity for a key is 25 years.

For each key that you generate, you're given a certificate that contains all the information about you and your company. You don't necessarily have to fill in all the details—just choose the ones you think should go on your certificate. A key will still be generated, even without filling in each field of the certificate.

Finishing Up
Once you have filled in the details for the certificate, select OK. You will then be directed back to the Generate Signed Bundle or APK screen.

Here, all of the fields will now be pre-filled for you. Go through all the details to stay on the safe side. Then, select Next.

Figure-16h

On the last screen, you will now be able to see the destination of your Signed APK file. Below that, you will see two more options: Debug and Release.

Debugging is used when the application is still in the testing phase. Since your application has passed the testing phase and is ready for deployment, select Release.

There are two more checkboxes towards the bottom of the screen. Select V2 (Full APK

Signature) and click Finish.

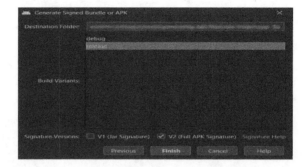

Figure-16i

You will be notified by Android Studio once the APK build is finished. Now, you can click on Locate from the notification to open up the file location.

The Signed APK file is named app-release.apk by default. You will find it in your project folder in the app/release directory.

Publishing App to Google Play Store

Ensure that when you have completed the work with your App, it is compatible with every Android version.

1. Open Google Play Developer Console.

2. Pay $25 for signing into the Google Play Publisher account.

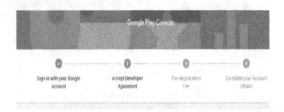

Figure-16j

3. Once you have paid, click on Create Application.

Figure-16k

4. Give a title to the application and click on Create.

Figure-16l

5. Give a short description and a long description. You have to give all the links and everything in the full description.

Figure-16m

6. Scroll down and give high resolution (1920*1080, 720*1280, 480*800) screenshots.

Figure-16n

7. You can drag it and rearrange its positions.

8. Scroll down and upload the high-resolution icon of your application.

9. Upload the Feature Graphic.

10. Now, add the promo graphic.

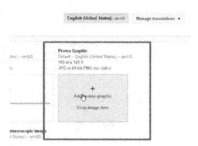

Figure-16o

11. You can add the TV banner and the new feature, Daydream 360-degree stereoscopic image also promo video instead of feature graphics.

12. Go to Application type and select Application from the drop down menu.
    Go to Category and choose a category for your application.

13. You can mention your website along with other details if you have one.

14. Click on the button if you did not submit any privacy policy.

15. Save the application as draft.

16. Click on Apk. Upload the Apk file.

17. You can also do the Beta testing and Alpha testing if you want to.

18. Click on Content Rating and click Continue.

19. Enter your email id.

20. Select your app category and fill in the questionnaire provided.

21. Click on Save Questionnaire.

22. Click on Calculate Rating.

23. When the rating is complete, click Apply Rating.

24. Click on Pricing and Distribution. Choose the 'Paid' or 'Free' version. You can change it later to Paid version if you are selecting the 'Free' version at present.

25. Select the countries.

26. If your app contains Ads, select Yes, else select No.

27. Scroll up to right corner and click on Save Draft.

28. Click on Publish app.

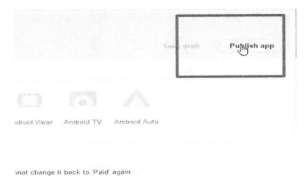

Figure-16p

29. The application is published. It may take around 2-5 hours for the app to be visible on Google Play.

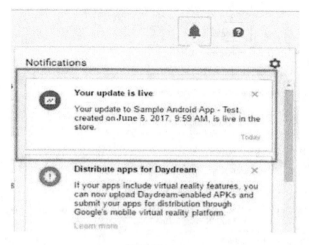

Figure-16q

Android Debug Bridge (ADB)

Android Debug Bridge or better known as ADB is a command line tool to access your Android Phone. It is a powerful and pretty versatile tool. You can do a range of things like pulling out logs, installing/uninstalling apps, transferring files, rooting and flashing custom ROMs, creating device backups, etc. Moreover, adb is a life-saver when your Android device gets bricked because the phone is unusable at that time.

Though the adb command shell looks intimidating and complex, it is fairly simple. So, here is a list of adb commands to get you started and do some useful things in the process.

Install ADB on Windows

Unlike in previous versions, you don't have to install a complete Android SDK to install ADB. Simply download the standalone ADB zip file, extract it to a folder of your choice, and you are done.

To access adb, open the command prompt by searching it on the start menu. To run ADB commands, you need to navigate to the adb folder using the below command.

cd C:\ADB

Where in C:\ADB is the folder location of the extracted ADB file.

Tip: You can also open the Command Prompt from the same directory. Just type "cmd" on the address bar in the Windows File Explorer Now, connect your Android device via USB and you can proceed to test.

Connection Commands

1. Start or Stop ADB Server

Obviously, the first command you should know is how to start and stop the adb server. This enables you to interact with your connected Android device. To start the adb server, use the below command.

adb start-server

Once you are done with your work, you can use the command below to stop the adb server.
adb kill-server

2. Restart ADB in USB Mode

If the ADB server is already started and for some reason, the commands are still not working. You can try an ADB restart on the USB. There is no standalone ADB restart command. But the following command will reestablish the ADB connection via USB. This, in turn, will cause the ADB server to restart.

adb usb

3. ADB Version

This is a very handy command because few commands work with the latest ADB versions. Like for example, the older versions of ADB don't let you run flashall command. So, when you have a command in error, the first step is to check the adb version. You can then verify whether the command is supported in that version. Following is the command to check the adb version.

adb version

4. List Connected Android Devices

This is one of the most famous commands. When you connect your device to the computer via USB, use this command to verify if adb can find the connected device.

adb devices

If your device is properly connected to your system, the above command will start the daemon service, scans the system and lists all the connected Android drives. The good thing about this command is that it lists both the state of the device and its serial number.

5. Status of Your Device

As you can tell from the name itself, this command can be used to know the device state. When the command is executed, it shows whether your device state is in offline, bootloader or in device mode. For a normal Android device, you will see your Android state as "device", just like in the below image

adb get-state

The connection state of the device can be one of the following:

> offline: The device is not connected to adb or is not responding.
> device: The device is now connected to the adb server.
> no device: There is no device connected.

6. Connect ADB over Wi-Fi

In the recent ADB versions, you can directly connect to any Android device over Wi-Fi. All you have to do is turn on USB debugging on the other device and run the following command.

adb connect ip-address

So the command should be like:

adb connect 192.168.1.104

7. Get Device Serial Number

This command lets you know the device serial number of the connected device. On your phone or tablet, you can see the device serial number by navigating to "Settings > About Phone > Status".

adb get-serialno

File Transfer Commands

8. List Files

In order to copy or send files, you need to know the exact location of the directory. Normally, the phone internal memory is named as sdcard. So, all the phone internal folders are under the /sdcard directory. Still, if you want to know the exact location or locate a particular file, you can use the "ls" command. ls command lists out the files under the directory.

adb shell ls "directory_name"

9. Copy Files from Computer to Phone

If you want to copy files from your computer to your phone using adb then you can use this command. Do forget to replace [source] and [destination] with actual file paths.

adb push [source] [destination]

Once you replace the above command with actual file paths, this is how it looks like. adb push "E:\Video Songs\sample-song.mp4" "/sdcard/Downloads/sample-song.mp4"

10. Copy Files from Phone to Computer

Just like you can copy files from your computer to Android device, you can copy files from your phone to computer. To do that simply use the below command. Replace [source] and [destination] with actual file paths.

adb pull [source] [destination]

Once you replace the above command with actual file paths, this is how it looks like.

adb pull "/sdcard/Downloads/video.mp4" D:\Downloads

App Installation

11. Install/Uninstall Apps

Besides from moving files back and forth, you can actually install apk files with just a single command. To install an app you have to specify the full path of the apk file. So, replace "path/to/file.apk" with the actual apk file path.

adb install "path/to/file.apk"

To uninstall an app, simply execute the below command. Replace <package-name> with the actual fully qualified package name of the app.

adb uninstall <package-name>

If you have multiple devices attached to your computer and only want to install the apk file on just one device then use the below command. Replace [serial-number] with the actual device serial number. You can get the device serial number using this command.

12. List all Installed Packages

Now, uninstalling packages would require you to get the exact package name. The package name is actually different from the installed app name. So, to find that below is the adb command.

adb shell pm list packages

Now the resulting output is pretty vast. So if you want to list a particular apk, you can try filtering by the app name. For example, I want to search the package name for FDroid, so I will use the following command.

adb shell pm list packages | findstr "fdroid"

Backup & Recovery Commands

13. Backup Android Device

To backup all the device and app data you can use the below command. When executed, it will trigger the backup, asks you to accept the action on your Android device and then creates "backup.adb" file in the current directory.

adb backup -all

14. Restore Android Device

To restore a backup, use the below command. Don't forget to replace "path/to/backup.adb" with the actual file path.

adb restore "path/to/backup.adb"

15. Reboot Android Device into Recovery Mode

The recovery mode helps you repair or recovery the Android device using the tools built into it. Generally, you can boot into recovery mode using the volume and power button combination. Alternatively, you can also connect your device to the system and use the below command to boot into recovery mode.

adb reboot-recovery

16. Reboot Android Device into Bootloader Mode

The below command lets you boot into bootloader mode. Generally, the bootloader mode is very similar to the fastboot mode.

adb reboot-bootloader

17. Reboot Android Device into Fastboot Mode

The fastboot mode is generally used to flash custom ROMs, bootloader, and even kernels. Use the below command to boot into fastboot mode.

adb reboot fastboot

18. List Connected Fastboot Devices

This is one of the lesser known commands. When you boot the device in fastboot mode, in order to check if the device is connected you can use the following command.

fastboot devices

19. Start Remote Shell

This command starts the remote shell and lets you control and configure your device using the shell commands.

adb shell

Utility Commands

20. Take Screenshots

It is nothing hard to take a screenshot on and Android. All you have to do is press the Power button and Volume Down button at the same time. Alternatively, you can also use this command to take a quick screenshot. Replace "/path/to/screenshot.png" with the actual destination path. If you want to, you can customize the file name by changing "screenshot" with whatever name you want.

adb shell screencap -p "/path/to/screenshot.png"

Once you replace the destination path, this is how the command looks like.

adb shell screencap -p "/sdcard/screenshot.png"

21. Record Android Screen

Apart from screenshots, you can record the Android device screen

using the below command. Again, replace "/path/to/record.mp4" with the actual destination path. Of course, you can customize the file name by changing "record" with whatever name you want.

adb shell screenrecord "/path/to/record.mp4"

www.ingramcontent.com/pod-product-compliance
Lightning Source LLC
La Vergne TN
LVHW051432050326
832903LV00030BD/3042